COLORLESS TRAGEDY

Nina Dow

(With The Hand of God, My Heavenly Father)

WestBow
PRESS®
A DIVISION OF THOMAS NELSON
& ZONDERVAN

WestBow Press books may be ordered through booksellers or by contacting:

WestBow Press
A Division of Thomas Nelson & Zondervan
1663 Liberty Drive
Bloomington, IN 47403
www.westbowpress.com
1 (866) 928-1240

ISBN: 978-1-5127-3476-8 (sc)
ISBN: 978-1-5127-3477-5 (e)

Library of Congress Control Number: 2016904232

Print information available on the last page.

WestBow Press rev. date: 01/17/2018

I would like to dedicate this book to my older sister, my mother and to all who deal with mental health issues. I would also like to dedicate this book to all who lost their loved one due to mental health. I hope that after reading this book that has God's Word in it fills your heart and soul. I pray that God will give you all peace and comfort.

C O N T E N T S

Introduction   ix

Chapter 1   The Day of Trial   1

Chapter 2   The Shock   20

Chapter 3   Back In Time   28

Chapter 4   The Pain and Loss   40

Chapter 5   The Test of Faith   51

Chapter 6   Life's Encouragement   57

Chapter 7   Letters of Love   63

Chapter 8   Life   71

About the Author   75

INTRODUCTION

I've written this book so that others will not have to go through the pain my family and I have endured. I hope by writing this book, which is my story, people will understand the importance of confronting mental health issues and dealing with them in a proper manner. My mission is to help save lives by exposing mistakes that we make by ignoring the warning signs.

One might ask why I chose the title, "Colorless Tragedy." I chose this title because anyone can be affected by mental illness. No nationality, race, gender or ethnicity is exempt from this disease.

CHAPTER 1

The Day of Trial

"God, I need to talk to you. I don't understand why this nightmare is happening to my family and me. Today, December 21, 2011, feels like the longest day of my life. It is a day that is moving in slow motion."

Waking up this morning, I looked out my bedroom window watching the raindrops fall, feeling scared and lonely. I was afraid and lonely because of the unknown, not knowing if I would ever see my mother again. My mom refuses to let us visit her in prison. "God, I'm not sure if this pain and heartache will ever go away. I know you said, 'I will never leave you nor forsake you.' (Hebrews 13:5) But tell me, why do I feel so alone, Lord?"

Okay! It was time for me to compose myself. I needed to look perfect when my mom sees me. I didn't want her to worry about me. She had enough going on. I needed to make sure the children looked perfect too. I wanted her to know they miss her and that it is not necessary for her to worry about them. But I was worried about their reaction to seeing her. She doesn't look the same as she had the last time they saw her. Mom has aged. She is very fragile. Not only does her soft skin look as if it could tear with the wrong touch, but she has also drastically lost weight. She still looks beautiful with her slick hair, a blend of gray and black, combed back with lots of waves through it.

I tried to prepare the children the night before by telling them that Nana looked a little different since they last saw her. "Please God, help me to keep it together for the children," I had prayed just before falling asleep.

There is a knock at my bedroom door. "Who is it?" I asked.

"It's me, mom," my daughter Samantha replied.

"Who?" I asked again. "Samantha!"

"Give me a minute," I managed to say. I wiped my face and fixed my hair. I opened my bedroom door. I immediately asked my daughter the big question. "Samantha, would you be willing to come with us to see your grandmother at the courthouse?"

"I'm not ready, Mom."

"But, you must understand, this may be your last chance to see her," I said.

She responded, "I am not ready, Mom."

I said, "Okay. Well, it's time for school. I'll drive you there."

While driving to school, I told Samantha that it was all right if she was not ready. Nana would understand. "Love you," I said.

Samantha responded, "I love you too. Mom?"

"What?" I asked.

"Tell Nana that I love her and miss her."

"I will."

I thought to myself that she loves her grandmother the way God loves us, unconditionally. John 3:16 says: "For God so loved the world that He gave his only begotten Son that whoever believes in him should not perish but have everlasting life." That's love, unconditional love.

When we arrived at school, I told Samantha to have a blessed day. I gave her a kiss on the cheek, and she closed the van door and walked into the building. I drove off wondering if she would be all right. She had made a big decision not to see her grandmother, knowing it could be her last opportunity ever to see her again.

I remembered Samantha's therapist telling me I couldn't force her to go to court. I thought who could ever imagine that a child would have to make such a decision. I couldn't imagine what was going on in her mind. I must get her to the therapist this week.

When I arrived home and walked into the house, I saw the rest of my children were ready. I looked at them and said, "I know it is going to be hard, but we have to be strong for Nana. I don't want her worried about us at all. She has enough to worry about; we have to look our best. "I think if she sees you all look amazing, she won't worry about you." I then told them what I had told Samantha. "This could be the last time that you ever see your Nana. So if there is something special you want to share with her, remember to do it quickly. We don't have much time."

They asked me how much time. "Five minutes," I said. "I know it's not much, but at least it's something." It has been more than a year since they have seen her. "Remember," I said. "Let's look our best." My son Jake asked if I would help him with his hair. So, as I brushed his hair, there was a knock at the door, and one of the children opened it. It was Richie.

Richie is like family to us. Richie is twenty-three years old. He is four years older than my oldest daughter. We call him our son. He walked in all dressed up very nicely ready to see Nana too. He got to meet my mom two years ago. He dated my oldest daughter Kimora for a few years. They even went so far as to become engaged. My mother was happy about the engagement.

She already looks at him as a part of the family. Whenever Richie and Kimora would visit her, she would make sure that there was a meal waiting for them. My mother always said that someday Kimora would be Richie's wife. Needless to say, that day has not yet come.

We were off to see my mother as Kimora drove I became scared, sad and worried. I was getting ready to cry, but I continued to tell myself that I have to hold it together for my children. "I can't cry now," I thought. "If my mom sees me crying, she'll worry."

The children asked if their therapist, Mrs. Sarah, would be at the courthouse. I said, "Yes, and she might be already waiting for us."

As we pulled into the parking lot near the courthouse, there was Mrs. Sarah. Everyone yelled, "Hi."

She waved and said she would wait for us at the parking lot entrance. We caught up with her and walked together to the courthouse. She asked the children how they felt about this moment. They all said "fine."

"You all look great," she said smiling.

The children replied, "Thank you, Mrs. Sarah."

"You look good too," I said. She was dressed in a black suit and her salt and pepper locked hair was pulled back into a ponytail. She had left a few locks out on her forehead like bangs. Security officers stood at the door as we entered. We had to take off our coats and put them and our other belongings up on the conveyor belt so they could make sure we were not carrying in anything that was not supposed to be in the courthouse. "This is how the courthouse officials keep everyone safe," I explained to the children.

Once the security search ended, we walked up the steps and into the elevator. We were to meet the lady at the Victim Protection Office. Her name was Mrs. McKay. Mrs. McKay was very helpful. She was one of the women who came to my home to tell me what had happened on the day of the tragedy. She has been a great support to our family from the beginning of all this sadness. The Office of Victim Protection works very closely with the District Attorney's Office.

We went to the office and saw Mrs. McKay and Mrs. Brenda. Mrs. Brenda also collaborates closely with the DA's Office. She knows how it feels first hand having a homicide in the family. She experienced the loss of someone very close to her heart, her son. Some guys shot and killed her son a few years ago. So she understands how my family and I feel. I must say; she is a tough lady having gone through a situation like hers and now helping others, who are dealing with the same type of situation, shows how amazing she is.

Mrs. Brenda and Mrs. McKay gave us all hugs. I introduced Mrs. Brenda and Mrs. McKay to Mrs. Sarah. I was glad they were there to support us. Now it was time to go upstairs to courtroom number seven. We all headed to the elevator, but Mrs. Brenda said she could not be in the courtroom for support because she had another case. She told us she was with us in spirit and would keep us in her prayers.

As the elevator door closed, I started to pray that God would make way for my children and me to see my mom without my dad and little sister. I wanted that time for my mother to spend with us because my little sister and father were able to see her more often than us through the year. I felt a lot of precious time lost. Replacing time is not an option, so I wanted my family to have a special time with her today.

I wrote a letter two days before the sentencing to the judge. Kimora and I took it to the courthouse so that the judge could read it. In the letter, I asked if she would allow us to have at least five minutes with my mother. I also asked if my mom could be put in a nursing home for life and not go to prison. I went on to explain in the letter that it would be cheaper for the State in which we live.

We finally reached the seventh floor where the sentencing would take place. We got off the elevator, and walked towards the courtroom; the District Attorney (DA) came to me and asked if my children would still like to see their grandmother? They said yes!

Then he asked if I would like to see my mother? I said yes! He said, "So you all would like to spend some time with her?"

I said, "If it is alright, we all would like to spend time with her because it may be our last chance to see her."

My mother would not allow me, or any of us, to visit her at the prison. I felt the reason she would not have us to visit was that she didn't want us to see her in such a terrible place. When I was growing up, my mother always told us, "If you ever get into trouble with the law, I will never come to see you in prison." She was always reminding me of that. I don't know why, because I was a pretty good kid.

The District Attorney was very nice to say we could see her. "How about I find out if it is alright for you all to see her in the conference room," he said. I was in shock. It took all my might not to cry.

When he came back, my husband was with him. My husband had arrived in the courtroom a lot earlier than us. The DA took us down the hallway to a large conference room. "I'll have the officers bring your mother to you," he said.

I know it might sound weird, but at that moment I could have given him a big hug. You wouldn't understand unless you dealt with what I had to endure. Just giving us a few minutes time spent with my mother was priceless. It was as if he had given us a gift.

I understood it wasn't his decision alone to let us see my mother; it was also the Judge's decision. All I knew was that this could be the last time I would be able to physically touch my mom's hand or give her a hug. It probably would be the last time I see my children speak to her, give her a hug, or a kiss on the cheek. God, please don't let this be goodbye.

Two officers brought my mother into the conference room. As I watched my children's reactions, my heart ached for them and my mom. The last time my mom had seen her grandchildren was the day before the tragedy. It had been a long time. I looked at my mother and said "hi," as the officers secured her wheelchair.

She was wearing a uniform; that was short sleeve orange top and orange pants with the initials of the prison on her back. She looked like she had lost more weight. I touched her hands. They felt so thin and fragile. I thought if I rubbed them too much the skin would tear easily. You could see my mother was weak at that moment, but she was still able to give her grandchildren a smile. I believe my mom was surprised to see them.

"How are you doing?" I asked. "Wait a minute, mom? What happened to your legs and feet? Why are they wrapped up all the way to your knees?" She said that her legs and feet were swollen and had sores on them.

"I'm alright," she said.

"Ok, Mom," I said. I didn't continue talking about her legs because I didn't want the children to worry. I told her I hoped she wouldn't be upset with me for arranging the meeting. The kids wanted to see her and to give her a hug. My mother said that it was all right that they were there because they wouldn't be allowed in the courtroom. She was clearly happy that I had brought them. She wanted to see them. Then I told them if they needed to say something to Nana, they should do it now because there wasn't much time.

Jake was the first to speak. He walked up to my mother and said "hi." He gave her a hug. She looked at him and said, "You are growing up. You have gotten taller. That is a nice suit on you." Jake smiled from ear to ear and nodded his head up and down. I thought to myself; my mother is looking at Jake as if she is taking a picture of him in her mind as if there are fears that she will not be able to remember him if she doesn't study every feature.

I think Jake was doing the same thing. I know it's hard for a little child to accept that his grandmother is in prison and possibly could be there until she dies. I'm sure he was trying to understand how a person with mental illnesses could be placed in a prison and not in a hospital. I'm sure he had come to realize that things would never be the same. There would be no more outings with Nana and his siblings. There would be no more holidays with his Nana. I knew he was in pain. The sad part about it was as a mother; I could not take away his pain.

Kelly was next. Kelly is my second daughter. She walked up to my mom. "Hi, Nana," she said. "We miss you a lot, Nana! By the way, I am wearing the sweater you bought me".

"Did I buy that sweater for you?" Nana asked.

Kelly nodded. "Yes, you did."

Nana said, "Well Kelly, that sweater looks good on you, and you've gotten taller. You're growing up."

"I'm taller than Kimora even though she is the oldest." Kelly smiled and whispered, "Nana, Kimora doesn't like being shorter than Samantha (my third daughter) and me."

Then Kimora gave Nana a hug. Nana hugged her too. She looked at the special praise and worship uniform Kimora was wearing and said that she looked pretty. Kimora thanked her and let her know that college was going well. She promised Nana that she would continue to make her proud. I could tell my mother was happy to hear that. She smiled, and Kimora hugged her again.

My mother asked about Samantha? I told her she wasn't ready to see her just yet. "She said to tell you she loves you and misses you very much," I said.

Kimora told Nana that Samantha had made a cake for her. Kimora took out her cell phone and showed Nana the picture. "Looks good, doesn't it, Nana?"

Nana looked at the picture and smiled. As I watched her eyes tear-up, I could tell it took everything she had inside not to cry. "It sure does," she said very softly.

"Nana, can you see what it says on the cake?" Kimora asked.

"It says I love you, Nana."

Kimora said "Yep. It was Samantha's first time making a cake on her own, and she made it just for you. She wasn't ready to see you, but she wanted you to know how much she loves you by making this cake," Kimora said.

My Mother asked what kind of cake it was. When I told her it was a yellow cake with icing on top, my mom said, "Tell Samantha the cake looks so good I wish I could have eaten it."

We all smiled, and she did too.

Standing behind Kimora was Richie. "Nana," Kimora said, "you remember Richie?"

She responded, "I didn't see you there. I didn't realize you were here. Richie loves my sweet potato pie."

Everyone in the room smiled. Richie said, "Yes! I sure do." He gave her a big hug. "It's good to see you, Nana."

"It's good to see you too," she said.

My husband walked towards her. He put his hand on her shoulder gently and said, "We're praying for you." She looked at him and thanked him for the kind words. He wanted to say more. I could tell. It was all over his face. But he held back. He was trying to hold back the tears, just like all of us.

Mrs. Sarah, the family therapist, introduced herself. She told my mother that she was helping us to deal with the situation. The therapist continued to say it was a pleasure to meet her. Mrs. Sarah let my mom know that she was a good grandmother. Mrs. Sarah knew all four of my mom's mental illness diagnoses. My mother thanked Mrs. Sarah for helping the family. Mrs. Sarah replied, "You're welcome, and it's a pleasure."

"It's time to go into the courtroom," the officer standing behind my mother's wheelchair said. All the grandchildren gave her a hug. I looked at my mom sadly and gave her a hug. Then I kissed her on the cheek as tears rolled down mine. I realized it could be the last hug or kiss I would ever give her.

The officer unlocked the brakes on the wheelchair. As he backed her out of the door, we all continued to say our good-byes. We walked behind the officers to the courtroom, and the tears that we were holding back could not hold any longer.

The courtroom was just a short distance away, but I felt like we had walked a mile in slow motion when we got to the door. Everyone continued to wipe away the tears. We had to be strong for my mother. One of the officers held open the door for her while the other wheeled her over to a table beside her attorney. My family and I sat in the back row on the other side of the room from where my mom sat; we were near large wooden doors. We chose to sit in a neutral area of the courtroom, not behind the DA or in the defendant's area. Either way, it did not matter. Our purpose for being there was to be supportive of my mother. Regardless of the bad mistake that she made, she was still my mom and Nana to her grandchildren, no matter what we still love her.

I was having back pains and noticed a cushioned chair nearby. I asked if I could sit there. Mrs. McKay and the Bailiff, a man who helps out in the courtroom, said it was all right. Once I sat down, I asked Kelly and Jake to leave the room. When they asked why, I told them, "We need to honor your grandmother; things said amongst the Judge, DA, and with her attorney that she will not want you to hear."

They went outside and sat in the hallway until the proceedings were over. Then we waited for the court session to begin. I noticed a lot of activity in the courtroom. People were entering and leaving, and I didn't know any of them. Mrs. McKay explained that the case was open to the public. In the midst of all the people coming and going, I learned that the press from the Sun News was there. I couldn't identify the press, but I knew they were present because later in the day I heard about my mother's case on the evening news. The following day there was an article in the newspaper and another on the Internet.

I looked over at my mother as she sat in the wheelchair and I could see the pain and sadness. She kept her head tilted down most of the time. My father, his close friend Mr. Bob, my little sister Gretchen and her husband Troy sat behind my mother and the attorney who was representing her. Unfortunately, division has arisen amongst us.

That was one of the reasons I chose to sit on the opposite side of the room with just my immediate family, to avoid conflict or confrontation of any kind.

The next thing I heard was, "Please rise for the honorable Judge." Everyone in the courtroom stood up. I looked around the courtroom and started praying silently, "God, I see the words liberty, justice, and honor. Right now, God, I am pleading for mercy and grace for my mother. God, the pain she caused hurts a lot, but it was because of her mental illnesses. She didn't mean it. I beg you. I am pleading with you God. Please have mercy on my mother. I have forgiven her. I know you have forgiven her. She didn't mean it."

I heard someone shout, "Be seated" everyone in the room sat down. The Judge did not come out of the chamber. So, I took my book of prayers and Bible verses out of my purse and started to read. Then I heard again, "Please stand for the Honorable Judge" so everyone stood. The Judge walked in and sat in her seat. The courtroom official said out loud, "Please be seated; the courtroom is now in session," everyone sat.

The Judge had questions for the prosecutor (District Attorney) which he responded too. When it was time for my mother's attorney to speak, he talked about concerns for my mom's medical condition brought on as a result of her shooting herself in the torso, which was an attempt to committing suicide. She was now partially paralyzed and needs a lot of medical care. "She has ongoing medical needs," her lawyer said, "physical and mental. She is unable to tell anyone when she needs to go to the bathroom because she has no feeling from the torso down to her feet. She has sores on both legs down to her ankles. She is unable to stand for extended periods of time. She can take a few steps only with the help of a walker." He doubted she would get the medical attention she needed in prison.

The Judge asked the attorney if he's finished. "Yes, your honor," he answered. She went on to say, "I have to follow the law. If only there was another way. But the law, as it is written, gives me no other alternative. It will be a big cost to the State, but the law is the law."

The Judge had previously sent my mother to the medical unit of a state prison for two months to have an evaluation done on her before sentencing. She read aloud the medical report. She said, "Upon reading the evaluation and having taken into consideration all that was said, two prisons would best suit her needs."

My mother's attorney spoke again about his concern for the care she would receive. The Judge said, "The prison that did the evaluation would be the best place for her."

Sadly, it was time for the judge to give my mom her sentence. The Judge asked sides, the prosecution and the defense if there was anything else they needed to say. Both sides said, "No, you're Honor."

At that moment, Mrs. Sarah asked my husband, who was sitting next to me; if it would be all right if she sat by me. He responded, "Sure." She sat beside me and held my hand as I looked straight ahead. From the corner of my eye, I could see Mrs. McKay (Victim Protection Advocate) looking back at me off and on. I guess maybe she wanted to see my expressions. Maybe she thought I would yell out in the courtroom.

I thought, just perhaps, the Judge would be willing to send my mother to a nursing home. I was hoping that she would allow her to go into a nursing home because I knew deep down in my heart that my mother would not allow us to see her in prison. Prison is not a place where a grandmother would want her grandkids to see her live her senior years, possibly for the rest of her life.

Then the Judge said, "Please rise," to the defendant. I looked over at my mother feeling like a little kid, scared, sad, and confused. Maybe she had the same feelings. My mother could not stand. She remained seated in her wheelchair, but her attorney rises to his feet.

I started to shake a little. I think it was the fear of knowing I might not ever see my mom again. A small part of me thought, with all the problems my mother has, she is not a threat to society anymore. She is now on the right medications and under constant medical care.

The Judge finally said the words I did not want to hear, "Life in Prison." My thought was life means forever. Such pain, shock, and hurt; I've never felt before. The unknown lays ahead for my mother and the family. Tears were in my eyes, ready to explode non-stop but somehow they didn't fall. I thought of my children. I just knew I had to stay strong for them.

I looked over at the therapist. She gave me a hug and said, "Hang in there." My husband looked at me. He knew I wanted to cry, to let it all out. He said, "Stay strong." Then he changed seats with the therapist as tears rolled down my cheeks and I wiped them away. My husband gave me a hug. I looked over to my mother. She was looking down into her lap. She looked so very fragile. How would she survive in prison? In her condition, I wondered how she would survive amongst the other inmates.

I looked at my dad thinking that he has never been without Mom. My mom has never been without him. They married at an early age, she was eighteen, and he was nineteen years old. They are both in their early sixties now and would have to learn how to live apart, a sentence unto death. It has been almost forty-five years of marriage for them. I couldn't imagine them apart. My father looked so confused and in shock with the verdict. It was weird. Again, I felt like everything was in slow motion as if time had to slow down for me to fully comprehend and process what was happening.

I lost my older sister who I love dearly. I won't see her anymore on this earth or in this lifetime. Now I lost my mother. I knew I could write letters, but it is not the same as having the person in front of you. For a moment, the little girl in me wanted to reach out to my parents. Then I heard, "Please stand!" Everyone in the courtroom stood as the judge walked out. I told my husband I needed to go outside the courtroom doors so that I could see my mother one last time.

The immediate family and I went outside and waited, hoping to see her, to get a final glance. The sheriff opened the doors as the other officers rolled my mother out in her wheelchair towards us. I kept my eyes on her as if I was taking a picture of her in my mind. She would never let us see her in prison. I believed it was her way of protecting us from the pain of seeing her at the lowest point in her life. I understood. No grandmother would want their grandchildren to see them in prison.

I think my mother was concerned with the impact it could have on their minds. She believed that if they didn't see her in jail, it would lessen the fears they had about what was happening to her behind the walls of the prison and I feel the same way. I could never image this happening to my mother; spending the rest of her life, her golden years, in prison. I always thought my parents would enjoy their retirement years together. My mom in jail for the rest of her life for killing her first born adult child, I can't believe this. Just hearing those words sounds ridiculous. Here I am in the hallway of the courthouse, trying to make eye contact with my mother, trying to get her attention, shouting "I love you mom" with tears rolling down my cheeks, nonstop, as the officers take her away to prison. My mother finally looked up at her grandchildren. They shouted, "I love you, Nana. I love you."

She just waved her hand goodbye. I knew my mother was holding back her tears as she waves. We all knew how much she wanted to give hugs and kisses to us all. I blew her a kiss as the officer rolled her away from me and down the hall. My heart ached so badly, in such a way that I can't describe. I lost my older sister from one bullet to the side of her head. Now I lost my mother to life in prison for pulling the trigger.

I was hurt because there was no way for me to go back in time and change this horrible tragedy. I was hurt and upset because my father would not allow my children and me to visit my mother in the rehabilitation hospital; all because of lies told to him by my little sister Gretchen. He knew that once my mom goes to prison, she wouldn't want to see us. It hurts so bad knowing that my father and little sister blamed me for all that had happened. I wasn't even around my parents' home for four months before the tragedy to avoid my mother and her bad behavior towards me. I was unaware of the series of events that took place that leads up to the tragedy. By series of events, I mean the fact that my mom was diagnosed with major mental illnesses before the tragedy and I was not informed of the issues nor when she was put into a psychiatric hospital. I asked Gretchen and Troy which hospital was our mom in and they would not tell me. They both said mom did not want me to know where she was. I asked my father the same question, "what hospital was mom placed in?" He would not tell me. I even called my mother's brother who lives in another town, asking him the same question. I thought maybe they would have talked to him because my mom was close to him. My uncle had no clue on what was going on. So the only people that knew at that time where my mother was placed was Gretchen, Troy, and my father. I didn't understand why they wouldn't let me know what was going on. I guess I will never get that question answered. So you see that I wasn't around because I was pushed away and excluded. There is only so much a person can handle when it comes to being pushed away. I finally got tired of being rejected, so I distance myself. Sadly to say, when my father left the courtroom, he did not speak a word to his grandchildren or me.

I want to explain why I would stay away from my mother at times. It was because I was tired of being put down in front of my children. No, I did not finish college or get the best paying job, but I love working with elderly and being a blessing to them. I also love helping children to the point that I knew God wanted me to adopt children. That may not be something fancy to talk about to some people, but that's all right with me. No, I did not marry an American man, but instead a kind gentleman from another country. I love my husband very much. I felt no matter what I did; I could not make my mother or father happy. It was more my mother putting me down than my dad. I was told, "just as long as you are doing what God wants you to do, and it makes you happy, then keep doing it." So I did! But in the process, I started shutting down. I slowly began talking less when I was around my mother; visiting her less until one day it came to a complete stop. I shut down because of the hurtful words and comments she would make towards me in front of my children. I know people say that words don't hurt, but they do, and it's hard to forget them. I thought it would be best to stop visiting as much. I never stopped my mother from coming to my house. I wanted her to have a relationship with my children. I allowed her to take her grandchildren wherever she wanted too. I love and honor my mother, but I never told her the reason why I wasn't coming over to the house as much because of her. I know my mom enough to say if I had told her the reason why I stop visiting her, she would have denied it.

Then the next day she would bring something to the house that she bought and said it is for the family or the grandchildren, this was her way of making peace. All I would want to hear was, "I am sorry, and I will not do it again." 'I am sorry,' are words you would never hear in my parents household. That is why I work very hard to teach my children it is important to say 'I am sorry' when they do something to someone, and it hurts that person feelings.

I, as a mother, say 'I am sorry' to my children if I say something and it hurts their feelings. As parents, our children need to hear these words. Hearing the phrase, 'I am sorry' from someone who loves you, shows how much respect and honor they have for you.

I love my father dearly. I don't understand why he would think the worst of me. I truly thought we had a close relationship. He would always come to see us. I miss my family. I love them too much to hurt them. I do not understand why he would shun his grandchildren, son-in-law and me over lies. On the other hand, why would Gretchen tell lies about me and destroy what family was left? I have a lot of "why" questions that just might never get answered. Only God in heaven knows the truth. In church, I was taught that darkness would come to light. (Luke 8:17) That statement means the truth will come out some day. It may not come out when you want it too, but God will bring it out somehow.

I remember how confused my father looked as he passed us in the hallway after the sentencing. He walked a few feet in front of us in the lobby and stood there. My family, Mrs. Sarah, Mrs. McKay and I walked towards the elevators together. As I passed my father, I said out loud "I tried." Then I continued walking to the elevator and pushed the button.

When I shouted out loud to my father, "I tried" I was referring to the letter I wrote to the Judge begging her to send my mother to a nursing home and not a prison. I was praying that the Judge would consider it.

As I waited for the elevator, I saw Mr. Bob. I thanked him for being at my father's side. He was a great support for my mother, too. It seems like in the toughest times of a person's life is when they find out who are truly their real friends. Sadly, it's the same way when it comes to family, you may have the title of a family member because of the blood going through your veins, but that is still not enough to be family, at least not to me. Families are to show love for each other in the good and in the bad times, that's called love. Never leaving, nor forsaking each other. God promises never to leave us nor forsake us. (Hebrews 13:5) But when it comes to men and women, who are human beings and who are imperfect, we must remember that sometimes they cannot keep that promise. Only God is perfect. Who wouldn't want to have God by their side? He is there for us no matter what the situation may be or how strong the storms are in our lives. We might get knock down, but with God, we don't have to stay down.

Having real friends by your side in hard situations is truly a blessing. Sometimes you can't express it in words, but having friends nearby to pick you up when you are down is very meaningful. Mr. Bob gave me a hug and said, "Hang in there." It meant a lot.

I worry about my mother. I worry about my dad just as much. He has never been without mom. The thought of him finally realizing that his wife is in prison for life and will not be by his side for the rest of his life is devastating. My dad doesn't cook so there will be no homemade meals. He was always a hard worker and a provider. He worked very hard to make sure his family lived in a good and safe neighborhood. My parents held traditional beliefs about the family. The wife stayed home with the children while the father worked outside of the home.

Mr. Bob knew I was worried about my dad. He was aware that I wanted to be there for my dad, but my father would not allow it, he'll reject me. So I was extremely glad when Mr. Bob told me he would check on him. I said, "I am happy my dad has you as a great friend."

Mrs. Sarah walked with us back to our vehicle. She gave us hugs and told me she would call us later to see how we were doing. I thanked her for taking time out to come to the courthouse. I was concerned about how my children were doing mentally? Today the sentencing marked the second time there was a significant change in their lives. Nana was going to prison.

When children think of a grandmother, their Nana, somewhere in their minds, they believe their Nana will be able to watch them grow up. Now my kids know for sure their Nana will not be there to see them grow up. It will be difficult to hear other kids talk about their grandparents visiting, bringing gifts and simply supporting them. Although my father chooses not to be in their lives, my mother doesn't have that choice.

On the way home, I asked my children how they were.

They said they were okay.

"Is that it?" I asked.

My little son finally spoke. He said that when we all got to the courthouse, he was afraid. I asked him what made him afraid.

He responded, "I didn't know what to expect. I thought Nana would be upset because we were there."

I asked if he thought she was angry. He said, "No! Nana was happy to see us."

Kelly said she was glad that she got to see her. "What makes you say that?" I asked. Kelly answered "Nana needed to know we had forgiven her. She also needed to know we would never stop loving her and that she will always be our Nana."

I responded, "Nana would always love her grandchildren."

Kimora was our driver. After a few moments of silence, she shouted, "Why they couldn't just put her in a nursing home, then we would be able to see her; if they could place her in a nursing home."

I said quickly, "The Judge had to follow the laws."

Kimora replied, "Mom! Nana is weak, partially paralyzed, in a wheelchair, has aged and is very fragile. She won't hurt anyone. It seems like they have put her on the right medicines. Did you notice how her voice sounds? It's very soft."

"You know what! I did notice that, Kimora! I think you are right about the medications."

"Hey Richie, you put a smile on her face," said Kimora."

"I was happy to see a smile on her face," said Richie. She still remembered how much I liked her cooking. I love her pies. I'm going to miss that." Richie had tears in his eyes, but he didn't cry. He might not have cried on the outside for us all to see, but you could tell he was crying on the inside.

Kimora had tears in her eyes. In a soft voice, I asked if she was ok. "What do you mean?" she asked.

"Do you feel like driving us the rest of the way home?"

'I'm alright," she said. "I don't need to pull over."

I think all of us were crying inside, but we all were trying very hard to be strong for each other. There was silence for a long while, and then I said, "We need to think of the good times. No need to think of the bad times. I know it's easy to say, but hard to do. We must try to be positive."

Jake said, "It was good to see a smile on Nana's face today."

"Yes, it was," I said. I thought to myself; I'm sure Jake will never forget the last time he saw Nana.

When we arrived at the house, I thought about how I would be able to keep my children happy. "Hey kids," I said. "Can we make tonight a movie night?"

They responded softly, "Okay Mom."

I called a friend who had picked up Samantha after school and asked if he would bring her home. He said that they weren't at his home but a nearby fabric store that he would drop her off once they left the store. Within five minutes Samantha was home. I opened the door and thanked him for bringing her home. He said it was not a problem. Then back out the front door, he went.

I asked Samantha, "How was school?"

"Good. I made an A+ on my test."

"That's wonderful," I replied. I worry about how all my children are doing in school. Samantha is doing a great job. I believe studying was her way of taking a break from all that was happening.

"How is Nana?" She asked.

I looked at her, and took her hand, and said, "She ended up getting life in prison. The Judge gave us about ten minutes to spend with her instead of the five minutes. That truly was a blessing. Nana asked about you, and she understood you were not ready to see her. She thanked you for making the cake too. Kimora showed her a picture of your cake. She said she wished she could have tasted it. Nana looked closely at the picture. I could tell she wanted to see all the details you put on it. She said it looked good."

The children told Samantha that Nana had lost a lot of weight. Kelly said she was a whole lot smaller than she had been.

"Nana has a lot going on right now. I guess the weight loss is to be expected," I said.

Jake told Samantha that Nana smiled when Richie spoke to her about her cooking.

I could see that Samantha was upset. She looked sorrowful. Her eyes filled with tears, so I said in a pleasant voice, "Everyone, let's take off our good clothes and put on play clothes." Everyone went to their bedrooms to change.

Richie had to go to work. He thanked us for allowing him to come with us to see Nana. He said he was happy he had gotten to see her. I told him I would talk to him later and to have a good day at work.

I went into Samantha's room. I asked if she was all right. She started to cry. I asked what was wrong and she said she didn't get to see Nana.

"Samantha," I said. "I told you to go with us."

"Mom, can I go and see her now?" she said. I put my arms around her. "Samantha, do you remember what I said earlier?"

"Yes. You said it might be the last chance I get to see Nana."

"That's right," I replied. "I'm sorry, honey. But Nana will not allow us to go to the prison to see her. She doesn't want us to see her in there. Samantha, Nana understands it was too much for you. Nana will always love you. I want you to remember its okay to talk about her and all the fun times you had with her. Nana would like that. Now, if she changes her mind and lets us visit her in prison, we will go. But don't count on that. I know my mother won't do that. If she does, it will be a surprise to me. C'mon, let's watch a movie."

"Can we watch something that's funny?" Samantha asked.

"I think that would be good for us all." I gave her a big hug with a kiss on the forehead and told her to change her school clothes and put on her play clothes while I prepared dinner.

As I left her bedroom, there was a knock at the front door. My husband stood at the door with bags of groceries in both arms. He put the groceries on the kitchen table and asked how I was doing. I reply, "I'm hanging." Tears started rolling down my cheeks like a waterfall, non-stop. I quickly wiped them away over and over again.

When he asked about the children, I responded, "Same as me, trying to hang in there. The kids are going to watch a movie to calm down. I even made sure it is a funny movie. I don't want to see teary eyes like mine. So they're going to watch a funny movie to put some smiles back on their faces."

My husband said that it would be good to put their minds on something else for a little while. He looked at me. "Are you sure you're okay?" he asked.

"No!" I said. "I'm not okay." He gave me a big hug. I told him I loved him. I thanked him for being with me. "I didn't think you would be able to get off from work to come to the courthouse, but you did."

"God made a way for me to come," he answered.

"Thank you," I said. I needed to get dinner ready. I went into the bathroom and washed my face because my makeup was running everywhere. I closed the door and sat down on the toilet seat. In a whisper, I asked God, "Why? I just don't understand. Why God? Help me understand. How do I make sense out of this?"

My husband knocked on the bathroom door. "Is everything alright?"

"I'm all right," I replied.

"Don't you think I know you by now?" he asked.

"What do you mean?" He told me to open the bathroom door. "No. I'm alright. I'm just washing my face and hands," I said as the water was running in the sink. "I'm alright," I yelled again.

Finally, I opened the bathroom door, and my husband was still standing there. "You're not fine."

"I've got to be okay. I've got to be alright. I must be strong for our children."

"I know you do," he said. "I know you do, but it's alright to cry. Just don't get stuck in the sadness."

"I won't. I need to be the best mommy and wife I can be." I gave him a kiss and said, "Thank you."

"Stop thanking me," he said walking down the hallway. "But you're welcome," he laughed.

I hurried to the kitchen to start dinner. I thought to myself; God won't put more on us than what we can handle. As I was cooking, I heard laughter in the family room, and I felt so much better.

When I finished cooking dinner, I sat down with my children and watched the last fifteen minutes of the movie. It was pretty funny, and I was able to smile.

Everyone helped set the table for dinner. We sat down to eat, but first, my husband gave thanks to God for our food and many blessings. No one spoke a word about what had happened in the courtroom earlier in the day. Everyone talked about something else. I don't know why, but it was certainly all right with me.

Once dinner was complete, the family cleaned up the kitchen and dining room. Throughout that time there was no fussing or arguing about who was to do what. That never happens. That was a moment I'll never forget. But the real shocker came when they went straight to their homework after cleaning up and then prepared their clothes for school the next day.

Later that night, after tucking in the little ones and saying good night to the older children, I went into the living room and sat on the sofa. I placed a small throw blanket on my lap and put the Bible on top. I probably stared at the cover for at least ten minutes before opening it to Psalm ninety-one. It was a scripture taught to me, reading it in times for asking God to keep us safe. I read aloud: "He who dwells in the secret place of the Most High shall abide under the shadow of the Almighty.

I will say of the Lord; He is my refuge and my fortress: my God; in Him, I will trust." I read the entire ninety-first Psalm aloud, and I asked God to keep my family safe. I asked Him to keep my father safe and to let my little sister know how much I miss the little sister I use to know. I prayed that my fragile mother would be safe in prison as I lay on the sofa and cried and cried until I fell asleep.

CHAPTER 2

The Shock

"God, it's me again! I feel that I've been a big pain to you. I was taught talking to you and calling on you is not a bother because you love your children. I also was taught that we are not to just call on you in trouble. We are to have an actual relationship with you that means we can pray, talk about anything, cry, praise you, worship you in song and take time every day to be reading your Word, the Holy Bible. I feel like I am becoming more of a bother to you. Please forgive me if I am. God, I still can't understand why this happened to my family. I continue to play this tragedy over and over in my head, hoping for an answer to jump out at me."

July 26, 2010, is a day I will never forget. Early that morning, my dad knocked on the front door like always, so I welcomed him in. He had a cup of coffee for me in one hand and a newspaper in the other. He went into the kitchen to put the coffee on the counter and gave me the morning paper. I thanked him and then asked about everyone in his household. He said, "Everybody's alright." I shared with him what the children did the day before, and I told him that they were still asleep. I said that my husband was at work.

Then my dad said, "I better get home" as he walked towards the door, I thanked him again for the coffee and newspaper. "See you later, buddy," he said.

"Alright," I responded, then out the front door, my dad went and back in his vehicle to go home. It was my dad's routine every day. If there were no knock at that door in the morning, I would get worried. When my dad comes over every morning to check on us, that's his way of saying he cares about us. Dad always asked what project my husband was working on around the house. It was just another way he showed his fatherly love towards all of us. I miss that.

My mother had shown her love to us in other ways. Mom would take the grandchildren out to grocery stores, the mall, arcades, movies, parks, different restaurants and she even took the time to cook dinner for our family at times. Now there were times she would ask me to go along with them which I did, but eventually, her talk turned into insults, and that's when our times together slowly faded.

"God, I am so confused, I don't understand why my father is shunning my family and me. I was taught as a little girl in church that God is not a God of confusion. In the Bible, it says; 'For God is not the author of confusion but peace, as in all the churches of the saints.' (I Corinthians 14:33) I thought we had a close father and daughter relationship. I did not do anything to hurt my dad. I love him dearly. God in Heaven, tell me why? Why did this painful act have to happen in my family? A tragedy like this is something you watch on a television show like CSI. This horrible act is irrational.

Let me take you back to the day of July 26, 2010, the day that changed the lives of my whole family. My husband was driving home from work when he received a phone call on his cell phone from my oldest daughter's godfather. Kimora's godfather is a very special guy with a beautiful family that we all love very much. He lives right down the street from my parents.

The reason he called my husband was to say in these exact words, "There was a shooting at your wife's parents' house. The police have closed the road so that traffic cannot go through."

My husband immediately called me at home. "Are you sitting?" he asked.

I said, "No, why?"

"There was a shooting at your parents' house."

"Dad just left," I said. "Are you sure?"

He said, "Yes. Kimora's godfather is on the other line right now. He's trying to find out what happened."

"Alright," I said. Then I hung up. But my husband was still on the other line. I clicked over again.

"Maybe there was a break-in or something," he was saying.

I yelled, "I got to go! I need to make sure everyone's alright." Then my husband asked me to wait. "I am on the road," he said. "I will be right over, in a little bit." He asked me to promise, to wait until he arrived.

The doorbell rang. I told my husband someone was at the door and that I needed to go. I hung the phone up on my husband, to open the front door. I saw four people dressed in very professional, business-like clothing and with distressed faces. I recognized one of the ladies because she is a friend of the family.

One of them asked if they could come inside and talk to me. I opened the door to allow the people to come in my home. I was still in the clothing that I slept in the night before neither was my hair done. I did not care how I looked at that moment. I just knew whatever they had to say was vital, because when I looked into their eyes, I knew something was wrong. I felt a weird feeling come over me.

I spoke quickly asking them to wait in the living room for a minute because my children, and the children my husband and I were planning to adopt, were in the house. I felt like whatever they needed to say was not good. I could tell by the look on all their faces. Then I yelled to my daughter Kelly and asked her to please take the children out back to play.

On this day, my daughter Samantha was not home because she had spent a few days with a friend. I asked Kimora to go out back also. I thought maybe I could tell her later with Kelly. But Kimora replied, "I am not leaving this room." I yelled to my son Jake, who was standing near, go on out back with everyone and play, which he did.

It wasn't a problem to have the children outside in the backyard because the weather was beautiful. There was lots of sunshine but I knew the news the ladies had come to share with me was not nice in any way.

They said that I should sit down.

"I'm okay," I responded. I remember a lady saying, "No, you need to sit down." I sat on the loveseat in my living room. I felt like something was wrong. One lady kneeled down in front of me and made eye-to-eye contact.

She said, "There was a shooting at your parents' house." There were shock and disbelief at what she said next; "Your mother shot your oldest sister in the head. I am so sorry your sister did not make it." She continued, "There is something else, your mother turned the gun on herself and shot herself in the torso."

I broke down and cried non-stop. My daughter Kimora was in tears too! Kimora said out loud, "No, this can't be!"

The front door opened, it was my husband. One of the ladies shared the shocking news with him.

I finally asked about my dad. "Where is my dad? Is he hurt? He just left here, not too long ago."

The lady said it was my Dad who found my mother. "He is alright."

"Can I see my sister?" I asked.

"She was taken down to the coroner," one of the ladies replied.

I responded, "My sister?" I was in shock. I was trying to understand, but I was very confused about it all. Just hearing someone tell me that my oldest sister is dead was unbelievable to me. I wanted to see my sister to prove them wrong and say they made a mistake. See, my sister is still alive; I wanted to tell them.

They said I could not see my sister until the autopsy is complete.

I asked, "How long would it take for the autopsy to finish?" They were unsure. "Where's my mom?" I asked. The response was that they took her to the hospital. Then I asked, "Where is my dad?"

"He is at the police station," someone responds. I asked, "Why?" The response was, "The detective has questions to ask him."

"My dad just left my house. No! No!" I responded. One of the ladies said that Dad was not in trouble. They were just trying to figure out why my mother would do this.

I was starting to feel sick to my stomach, and my head was pounding. I could not stop crying. I said I needed to use the bathroom and wipe my nose. I forgot to use my manners, to excuse myself in a nice way. At that moment I didn't think about manners. I was just heartbroken and in shock.

I walked back to my bedroom where there is a powder room. I put the toilet seat down to sit on it while I wiped my tears and cleaned my nose. My husband was still in the living room talking to the people about what happened. I looked up towards the ceiling as tears continuing to flow down my cheeks and said, "God, how can this be?" Then I put my face down in my lap with both hands over my mouth, crying and asking myself why did she do this? My mom loved my sister. I broke down crying uncontrollably. I got on my knees, begging God for an answer. "Why? Why?" I could not believe this? I continued to cry out to God.

My husband came to me and said we need to go to the police station. So I went back into the living room with my husband as the tears continued to flow down my face. The ladies all gave me a hug and said how sorry they were. I said that I just don't understand because my mom loves my sister. I asked them why she would do this. Their response was that it was what all of them are trying to figure out. Then a lady said that I needed to get to the police station. I said, "Alright."

The ladies wanted to drive us there, but my husband said he would drive me there. Kimora went out back to bring in the younger children. When they came inside from the backyard, the kids asked, "Who were those people?" "Your father and I will talk to you later about whom they are and why they were here," I said.

Kimora told me she needed to go with us. Kelly asked, "Is everything all right?" I said we would talk about it when I get back home, but for right now I need you to help babysit the smaller children." Kelly said, "I don't mind watching them but could I at least know why you was crying?" I responded, "Later alright? I love you, Kelly, and I promise when we get back I'll let you know what's going on, but I need to leave now."

I was still in my nightclothes, so I went to my bedroom to change. I put on a pair of jeans, t-shirt and brushed my hair back quickly into a ponytail. I think that was the fastest that I've ever gotten dressed in my whole life.

On the road to the police station, we called our pastor. We had him on the speaker phone. My husband and I both told him what had happened. The Pastor asked us where we were. My husband said that we were in the car on the road headed to the police station. Our Pastor said he would meet us there. Then he asked is it all right with me if he would be with us for support. I responded, "It's okay." He said he'd see us soon.

When we arrived at the police station, we went to the receptionist's window and told her our names. She asked us to take a seat in the lobby. "The detective will be with you in a few minutes," she said, so we all sat down.

Pastor asked me if I knew why my mother would do this. I said, "No, my mom loved my sister. They were very close. I just don't understand."

Meanwhile, Kimora was trying to reach my little sister Gretchen and her husband, Troy. She e-mail, text and telephone, but she could not contact either of them, and this is unusual because normally one of them is available, or they would say they would call you back. My pastor asked how many sisters and brothers I had. I told him there were four of us. I named them in order starting with my oldest sister Marie, who had just passed away. I said, I am the middle child, and then there was my little sister Gretchen who lives in New Jersey with her family. I went on to say that I had another sister who was born before the youngest sister, but she had died at seven weeks old on Thanksgiving Day. Pastor asked how she died. I told him, "Pneumonia."

I said that my mother was never the same after her death. Every Thanksgiving Day she would be sad. She always would make a big dinner and make sure we all were at her house on that holiday. She never wanted to have Thanksgiving Dinner at any of her children's homes. If we did not come to her house Thanksgiving Day, she would be upset and not talk to us for a little bit. Her not talking to us for a little bit of time is how we knew when she wasn't happy with us.

Finally, the detective came out into the lobby where we all were. He introduced himself and asked if my husband and I would come back to the room where they had my father. I said "Yes." I asked if it would be alright for my pastor to come back with us. I assumed my daughter would be allowed to go along with us, but the detective said, for now, my husband and I was the only ones they wanted at that moment. Kimora waited in the police station lobby with Pastor.

I was worried about my father. I couldn't imagine what he was going through mentally and emotionally. Who could ever imagine coming home and finding their love one had attempted suicide and as a result was now paralyzed from the torso down to the feet? Then dealing with the passing of their oldest daughter and finding out that her death was caused by her mother shooting her in the head.

The big question everyone wondered: Why are there guns in the household? Initially, the guns were in the house for protection. No one thought about removing them when my mother was diagnosed with mental illness. My father was heartbroken and upset with himself because he hadn't removed the guns from their home.

A law should be pass that no guns are allowed in the homes or vehicles of persons with severe mental health issues. I wish the law would state that no guns be allowed for anyone unless they are a part of law enforcement or the military, but we all know that will never happen. It's just a wish.

I was also concerned that my father might have a heart attack. This situation is just too much stress for anyone to handle. My dad did not just lose his firstborn daughter but also his wife, and all on the same day. Life would never be the same for him.

My husband and I walked into the room where my father was sitting. I walked up to my dad and gave him a hug. I asked him how he was doing as I hugged him tightly. He responded that he was hanging in there. He looked confused and puzzled.

Then this question was asked by the detective, "Why did your wife shoot her daughter and then turn the gun on herself." My dad was confused, broken-hearted and did not know the answer. None of us could understand how something like this could happen in our family.

We all knew my mother loved her daughter. The detective had asked my dad lots of questions before my husband, and I arrived in the room.

The detective asked what time my father was at my house that morning. I gave him the time. Then he asked if that was my dad's routine every day? "Yes, it is my father's routine every day," I replied. I continued to say, "It was my way of knowing that everything was alright with him. Also, it was his way of making sure that his grandchildren and I were doing fine."

Dad always asked about what kind of project my husband is working on at the house for that day. Sometimes he would come back later that day to help out with the project. I consider that being his way of bonding with us all.

The detective's next question was if I have seen my mom lately. "I haven't been over for a while," I explained. "I sent my children to my parents' house yesterday (July 25, 2010), along with Richie and Kimora to ask if she wanted to go bowling with them. The children told me she would not open the screen door. She told them she was not feeling well. They said 'Nana had a tissue over her mouth and nose.' They continued to say 'Aunt Marie (oldest sister) was also at the door standing behind her.' My mother told them that she did not want them to catch whatever she had."

The detective asked, "Where is Gretchen?"

I told him, "We are still trying to contact her."

Soon it was time to go. I quickly asked in low tone voice, "Where's my mother?" The detective lets us know which hospital they took her too.

My mom hadn't been charged with homicide yet. My Dad and I wanted to know when we could see Marie. The detective told us we have to wait until after the coroner had conducted the autopsy.

As we were walking out the door of the room where they had us, my cell phone rang and on the face of it was my little sister's number. I remember giving the phone to my dad. The phone was on speaker, so we all overheard what was said. Dad told her, "Your mom shot your sister Marie. She killed her!" I could see my dad's pain and hear it in his voice. I remember him shaking his head back and forth as he held the phone to his ear.

We all could hear Gretchen screaming into the phone to Dad, "I told you. I told you!" Along with those words, there was a lot of screaming and unnecessary comments made.

I never understood why she said those words. Then they talked about her coming to our parents' house, and the conversation ended.

I didn't know what my mother's illnesses were at this time. When she had been admitted to a mental hospital earlier, for some reason my father and little sister kept all that from me. My brother-in-law Troy told me later that my mother did not want me to know.

CHAPTER 3

Back In Time

In the early part of 2010, my mother called the police and told them that my husband had murdered my children and me. She was very upset. In my mom's mind, she thought it was true. The police called me to see if my kids and I were all right. I told the police that we all were fine. I asked him why they thought something was wrong. The police replied, "Your mother called 911, saying that your husband hurt you and the children."

I thought perhaps the officer had incorrectly heard my mother. I asked what he meant by "my husband hurt us." The police officer said, "Your mother thinks your husband murdered you all." I was surprised and shocked at the same time. I told the officer I had not been at my parents' house for a while. The last time I had visited with them was Christmas Day or the day before Christmas. We exchanged gifts but hadn't stayed long because my little sister and her family were there.

Gretchen and her family now live closer to our parents. In the past, they had been stationed far away because her husband is in the military. Now they were closer and could visit more often. I felt that maybe my mother wanted time just with my little sister and her family. At the last family gathering on Thanksgiving Day, she seemed so upset with my children and me.

On Thanksgiving Day, my kids had tried to set the table, and I had tried to help her cook the meal along with my little sister. It seemed like everything we did was wrong.

She would yell at the children if the napkins weren't folded to her liking. When I tried to solve the problem by saying I would fold the napkins, she said in a mean tone of voice, "No, give it to me. I'll do it myself." My children's feelings were hurt. They wanted to help their Nana. Also, it was embarrassing for them to be treated that way, especially in front of their Papa, cousins, aunt and uncle.

My little sister was helping to cook for the family. I decided to join in when I saw Gretchen cooking. I started dicing the onions that are going to be used in one of her homemade dishes. Mom yelled, "Give me the knife. You don't know how to do it right."

I said, "Mom, this is how you dice onions."

She got mad and said, "Just sit down! Your sister is doing it right. You don't know how."

When mom let Gretchen cook the meal, I was shocked and hurt. Mom would never, ever let us cook in her kitchen, regardless of our age. We could only stir the food, or at best, be her taste testers.

She was the mom, and it was her kitchen. But now she had allowed my little sister to cook and take charge in her kitchen.

So I did what I was told. I sat down, but I also shut down. I didn't speak unless spoken too. It was something I did a lot around my mother. When she would ask my kids and me to go places with her, I would say, "I won't be able to go, but you can take the kids," and she would.

I now know that shutting down was not the answer. But for me, at that time in my life, it was. Keeping the peace was all I wanted to do. I knew that if I went anywhere with her and the children, any remark that I made would result in embarrassing comments, said in front of my kids. The put downs were nothing new to my husband and me. They happened again and again. Many times after the children returned from a shopping trip or a fun outing with their Nana; they would tell me the negative comments she had made about us. But, I honor my parents regardless of what is said. The Bible says to honor your mother and father. "Honor your father and your mother, that your days may be long upon the land which the Lord your God is giving you." (Exodus 20:12)

After my mom had finished putting up a fuss about how the napkins need to be folded a certain way and the onions diced, she sat across from me making weird laughing sounds. My mother never acted that way before. The only word I can use to explain how she looked was strange then she was laughing to herself, which sounded like an animal. Sorry, but that's the only way I can explain it. I kept looking back and forth between my mother and Gretchen to see if Gretchen would turn and look at me, but neither one of us said a word about it. Yes, we probably should have questioned her about that behavior.

I decided after dinner my family, and I would help wash and dry dishes and then go home. I figured since Gretchen had not seen my parents in a while, it would be a good time for her to have time alone with Mom and Dad. Since my little sister's husband, Troy is in the United States Army; they live a military lifestyle.

The Thanksgiving Holiday has always been special to my family. If we didn't have dinner at my parents' house, my mother would be upset with me. When my little sister and her family lived far away, a phone call on that day would suffice.

As mentioned earlier, one of my parents' daughters passed away on Thanksgiving Day years ago. She was the third of my mother's four daughters. She died at the age of seven weeks old. She was very ill with pneumonia. Mom said she was a beautiful baby with a lot of hair. The death of my seven-week-old sister left my mother heartbroken. I don't think she ever really healed from losing her child. I believe Thanksgiving was more than a celebration based on history. It was a way of celebrating the child she had lost. I believe it is the reason she would become upset if we weren't at her house for Thanksgiving Day. The loss of a child of any age is tough for a parent to handle. I think it is even harder when the child is an infant. I feel my mother should have sought counseling to deal with the passing of her baby girl. I believe counseling would have helped my father also. I was very young when this happened.

The policeman, who called the house after my mom made the 911 call, said that my mom might have dementia. He said some people with mental illness had made phone calls like that to his office before. The callers would say things that were not true, although they believed them to be true. Later they would find out that the person had dementia.

He asked how long it had been since I visited my mom. I told him how long it had been, and that I had been busy taking care of my children. He said, "Maybe you should go over today to check on your mother." I said I would do that and let her know the children and I were fine. He said, "Maybe seeing you will make her stop thinking bad thoughts."

I thanked the officer and hung up. Just as I put down the phone, the doorbell rang. It was my dad. He asked if everyone was all right. I said, "Yes dad, you were just here!"

My dad said, "Good. Your mom wouldn't believe me. She called the police."

I told him about the police officer's call. "We're all fine," I said. "I'll go over to see what is going on with mom. Maybe seeing me will assure her that everyone is alright." My dad went home to see how mom was doing and to reassure her that we were all okay.

I drove to my parents' house, pulled into the driveway and everything seemed fine. I got out of my car and went to the side door, which was already unlocked. I walked in and yelled, "Mom!" I rushed through the kitchen and towards the hallway.

My older sister Marie yelled, "Mom's in here." Mom was sitting in a high back chair in the foyer near the hallway. There was a large mirror hanging on the wall behind her. Marie was standing beside our mom, and it looked as if she was trying to comfort her.

I asked Mom if everything was okay. She did not say anything and had a weird look on her face, her hair was uncombed, and she looked confused and disoriented. I asked Marie if everything was all right with mom because the police said she had called them about us being hurt by my husband. Marie said she knew about the call. Mom interrupted us and asked about the children. I stated that they were at home and reassured her that everyone was fine. I told her that I had been busy with the children and fostering other kids. I explained that the children have been very active in sports and other summer activities. I asked her why she didn't just come over like you used to do. She replied, "You won't let me."

I said, "Mom, I never said you could not come to my house. I never said you could not come and see the children. You know you can do that any time you want." I told her that Dad comes over every morning and sometimes more than once a day. "My husband and I have never had a problem with you visiting. You're always welcome!"

She continued to say, "You won't let me," over and over again. And each time I spoke, she seemed to become more and more upset.

I was not sure what was going on with her, but I knew for sure she wasn't in her normal state of mind. She was not herself. I didn't want to argue with her, so I said, "Mom, you can see that I am alright. The children are at home, and they are fine too."

I asked mom if everything was all right with her. "No!" she replied. I asked her to tell me what was going on. She said, "You did not come over or bring the children over."

I responded, "Mom, you were busy with Gretchen and her family. I was waiting for you to call or come over on your own. Mom, I'm only two to five minutes away. It's not like you couldn't come over. You could have called me. I am only a phone call away." I asked Marie, "Why hasn't she just called me? Dad comes over every morning, and he didn't say anything to me about mom being upset with me for not coming over. When dad comes over, he seems fine. He knows that I'm watching the younger children with the help of my older children."

My kids enjoy having the foster children at the house. It gives them someone to play with, and we have bonded with them. My husband and I have decided to adopt them. We love them as if they are already family. I'm at home or attending the children's sports activities. If we're not at a basketball game, then we would be church helping out. I looked at my mom and Marie and said, "I am sorry if I upset you. I didn't mean too."

My older sister said she wasn't upset. "It's only mom," she said.

I looked at my mom and said, "I am sorry." She did not respond. She just looked like she was out of it. Mom was not herself. At times she seemed to stare off into space. She looked very confused and uncertain about what was going on.

I could tell that she was worried, but it was not the regular kind of worry. I could hear the fear in her voice as she spoke and hesitated after each word. My mom's uncombed hair bothered me also because it looks like it was not combed for a few days. It was not like her. Mom always tried to look her best whether at home or if she went out somewhere.

When I went back home later in the day, I felt like something was wrong with her. I thought about what the policeman had said about the word dementia. I decided to call my little sister Gretchen to let her know what was going on with our mother. When I called, I told her I felt she was needed at home as soon as possible because something was just not right with mom. I figured she would be a big help because she had gone to college and had taken classes on stuff like that.

Gretchen and her family arrived at our parents' house later that evening. When they arrived, it was my brother-in-law who called and asked if I would come over and help out with my mom. I said that I would. I asked my daughter Samantha if she would go with me. I told her that she could play with her cousins. She agreed and jumped in the van, and as I was driving to my parents' home, something came over me. I felt like I needed to pray. I told Samantha that we should pray. I asked if she wanted to share a Bible verse before we prayed.

Samantha started saying the Lord's Prayer (Psalm 23), and I joined in with her, but I couldn't remember it word for word. I did not understand why this weird feeling of needing to pray just kept getting stronger. After Samantha had said Psalm 23, I prayed, "God give our family the wisdom to help my mother. Lord, please protect Samantha and me from all things that are ungodly. And please help this weird feeling go away, in

Jesus Christ's name, Amen." Samantha said, "Amen" too. We arrived at the house, and from outside, everything seemed fine.

The door was unlocked, so I went in and Samantha followed. My oldest sister immediately asked that Samantha stays in the bedroom with her cousins. I agreed.

The next thing I knew, my brother-law Troy and Gretchen were yelling at me. They said it was entirely my fault. They said the most hurtful, the meanest, and most disrespectful and unloving things imaginable. I couldn't believe what came out of their mouths. I did not understand why they attacked me and why they were saying things that were untrue.

I had great respect for Troy for many reasons, not just because he was in the military. After that confrontation, the respect I had for him has diminished. As for Gretchen, I realize that I spoiled her when she was younger. I treated her as if she were my child. I love her dearly. But the pain, the lies, the hurt and hatred that I received from her that day tell me I don't know who she is anymore. She is not the same little sister that I grew up knowing. I realize we change as we get older, but not like that.

I yelled at them. I told Gretchen and her husband I did not know what was going on with mom. They continued to yell at me as my mother and father watched in silence. I even yelled to my Dad for help, to stop Troy from yelling at me. We were almost nose-to-nose, with him spitting in my face. My Dad, the man that I thought I had a close relationship with, did not come to my rescue. I couldn't believe that my father allowed it to go on. It hurt when Samantha and her cousins, my nephews, came out of the room where my sister Marie had told them to stay and play. They heard all the noise and wanted to know what was going on. They walked into the kitchen where Troy was yelling at me as I tried to scream back to defend myself. I looked over at my daughter, and she seemed terrified. The cousins seemed confused as to why their father was yelling in their aunt's face.

I kept yelling, too. "I thought you called me to come over to help with mom. Instead, you are attacking me about things that make no sense."

But Gretchen kept yelling, "It's your fault. You know what you did."

And I kept asking, "What are you talking about, please, tell me what you're accusing me of."

She accused me, without a reason to back it up. She continued to repeat over and over again, "It's your fault," and "you know what you did." She would not stop repeating those words. It was as if she was trying to brainwash me into believing that I had done something wrong. I knew I hadn't. Trust me; the devil was busy that day!

The Bible teaches that the enemy (the devil) is an accuser. In John 8:44 it says; "You are of your father the devil, and the desires of your father you want to do. He was a murderer from the beginning, and does not stand in the truth, because there is no truth in him. When he speaks a lie, he speaks from his own resources, for he is a liar and the father of it." I felt deep in my spirit that something wasn't right with Gretchen. To make matters worse, while she was yelling, her children and niece (Samantha) are watching her poor behavior. Troy yelling at me got worse to the point I felt like he was treating me as a stranger and not family.

The next thing I know I am bent backward (he is a lot taller than me), and he was yelling the same words, but he soon changed the subject. "Your husband treats me like a little boy," he said abruptly.

"No, he doesn't," I said. "He respects you. I respect you. We pray for you all the time, even more, when you were across the seas."

He yelled, "No one told you to pray for me. I don't need your prayers."

I yelled, "We want to pray for you because we want you to be safe. We love you. If we didn't, we wouldn't have gone out of our way to send care packages when you were overseas."

Troy yelled, "I am not a boy."

I replied, "We never said you were a boy." He stated that my husband treated him like a boy.

"No, he doesn't," I said. I looked at my dad for help. "Tell them to stop this," I said, but my father said nothing and did nothing to calm the situation.

My mother was standing near my dad, and I went to her. I tried to give her a hug, but she punched and kicked me. Troy got between us, but my mom continued to punch and kick at me. I didn't hit back. She is my mother.

The police showed up at my parents' house and walked right into the house at the side door. There were an African American officer and a caucasian officer who were both men. I don't know who called the police, but I do know that they were not from our township. When Gretchen saw the african american officer, she knew his name, and they talked together for a minute. I remember her saying, "I hate that you have to see my mom like this." He responded that it's okay. As Gretchen was talking to him about our mother, I was wondering why they were here in my parents' house. I remember his name coming up in a conversation one time with Gretchen and her best friend. Gretchen asked him what he was doing with himself since their high school graduation.

The caucasian officer saw that my mother needed help and called the ambulance. Through all of my tears, I heard my mom say that she was fighting for her life. I didn't understand her statement, and I didn't know what was happening.

My mother was taken to a nearby hospital, and I thought it was best to take my daughter home. On the way home, Samantha cried out saying, "Mom, I thought they were going to kill you. I wanted to do something, but I didn't know how to help you, mom! I'm just a kid. I didn't know what to do. I wanted to help, but I thought they would hurt me if I tried." She couldn't stop crying. I cried with her.

When we got home, I gave her the biggest hug ever. I told her I was sorry that she had witnessed all the painful and hurtful actions from people in my family. "God is with us and watching over us," I said.

I could not fully comprehend what had just happened at my parents' house. I was as scared and confused as my daughter. But I knew my mom was ill, and at the hospital, she would get the help she needed.

When we arrived home, my husband was standing at the door. A few minutes later, my husband, my oldest daughter and I left for the hospital to be with the rest of the family. When we arrived at the hospital, there was still chaos. My mom was making weird statements about the governor. She said, "Please check my head. I have a metal piece that was placed in my head by the governor." She believed it. She begged the nurse and the doctor to take an x-ray of her skull, but that didn't happen. Her words might have sounded odd, even outlandish, but her words were a cry for help.

The hospital was going to send my mother home. They said my father should have her seen by a doctor the next day. Fortunately, my little sister intervened. She told the doctor that she was willing to sign papers to have her admitted as a patient. My father agreed as well. I thought it was a good idea also.

I left the hospital soon after that. I needed to check on my children, and later we went back to the hospital. My husband and I went to the emergency room to check in with the family to see how mom was doing. Everything with her was about the same, so we decided to go home again since it was getting late and there was nothing left for us to do. My dad and Gretchen felt the same way and told us to go home with the kids. So we did. I found out later from the hospital, after going back up there again the next morning that they kept my mother in the emergency room overnight. Then they sent her to a mental hospital and had her admitted. That was the only information they could give me. They couldn't tell me which hospital. My family did not bother to tell me what was going on with mom. I didn't understand what was going on with my Dad, Gretchen, and her husband and why they wouldn't tell me the name of the hospital.

I cried the entire way home thinking my children were going to be sad and confused about Nana. I knew they would worry and wonder about how they could help her. My mother felt that my kids were a big help to her when my little sister and her children lived further away. She would call thanking me for allowing my kids to come over and help clean her home. But if Gretchen and her family were around, then she would feel that my kids weren't a real help to her. When I was at the house, and I tried to help it seemed like nothing I did for her mattered or was right in her eyes.

I want to share some things about my mother that are out of the ordinary. When I told my mom and dad I was getting married, they did not agree with my decision to get married. It was one of the darkest times in my life. Not having my parents' support, and their decision to not be a part of my wedding day was sad. They missed out on so much. There are no memories and no pictures of them on that special day. My husband's family came all the way from another country to be at our wedding.

My parents didn't go to my little sister's wedding either. She lived in another state, and it was too far for them to travel. My dad will not fly in a plane because he is scared of flying, but my mother could have gone. I remember her flying to California to see her brother.

It's sad because my wedding was at a church that was on the same street as my parents' house. They lived only five houses from the church. That experience was painful, but I moved on and forgave them. I assumed they didn't attend the wedding because they were so attached to my oldest daughter Kimora. I had her before I met my husband and my parents loved her as if she were their child. They spoiled her a lot. My mom was there when she was born. She even cut the umbilical cord. She always reminded Kimora about cutting her umbilical cord when another family would visit. My mother was very proud to be a part of that. I am happy that she was able to experience cutting her granddaughter's umbilical cord because that was when the bond between them began. That was a special moment in both of our lives. Kimora and I lived with my parents for a while after her birth.

My husband took on a package deal, my daughter and I. She was only four years old when we married. I assumed my parents were upset because they felt I was taking away their child. My mom and dad were not happy that I had a child before marriage. I was considered an embarrassment to the family. My life during pregnancy was horrible with my parents. They were so angry with me that I wasn't even called by my name. I was called all kinds of bad names that were very hurtful. I know I let my parents down, but after Kimora was born, they fell in love with her.

Still, it was hard to make the decision to get married against my parents' wishes, but God gave me his approval. God gave me a good man. When my husband-to-be and I were dating, he was fantastic as a boyfriend, but most of all how he interacted with Kimora. I knew he would be a great father to her. I was shocked that he still wanted to marry me because my parents thought of all sorts of things to try to make him break off the relationship. They even went to his job and caused a commotion, which could have caused him to lose his job.

Believe me when I say that I was on an emotional rollercoaster. Some days I didn't know whether I was coming or going. I must say overall that it was worth going against their will and following God's will for my life. In the Bible, Genesis 2:24 says; "Therefore shall a man leave his father and mother, and be joined to his wife: and they shall become one flesh." My parents refused to talk to me for a little while that was to be expected from them.

I now wonder how much my mother's mental problems played in her decision to attend my wedding as for my father's behavior, he simply always agreed with my mom. There is an old saying that says; "happy wife, happy life." My dad had to live with my mom, so his goal was to keep peace in the household at least that's how I saw it.

Because of the special bond, my parents had with Kimora, my getting married, moving out and taking Kimora with me might have triggered my mother's behavior. She might have thought that I was taking away her baby. I've had time to think about this, and I believe that's what happened. In her mind, she wasn't looking at Kimora as a grandchild but as her child. The negative behavior developed because she felt threatened that the bond between the two of them would end. In her mind, my husband and I were taking away her child. It should have been a red flag (mental health issues) for the family, but we didn't know.

My mother's put-downs in front of my children went on for years. It got so bad that my older sister joined in. My mom and older sister would whisper back and forth in front of me. I felt that it was a bit weird, but after a while, I just felt that my mom didn't like me. Keep in mind; I didn't know that my sister Marie had mental health issues.

My husband didn't get off any easier, although they appreciated him coming over to help when something needs fixing around the house, they would still talk down to him and about him.

Even though my husband and I knew we were being degraded and talked about in front of our children, we would always tell them not to get upset. We would remind them to put their trust in God. In Proverbs 3:5-6 it says; "Trust in the Lord with all your heart, and lean not on your own understanding; in all your ways acknowledge Him, and He shall direct your paths." We always felt that God would work it out. And after a while, it was just easier to let the children hang out with their nana without me. But it didn't lessen the negative talk. She continued her negativity in front of them.

My husband taught me a lot about dealing with negative talk. He is really good with moving forth and not letting negative talk bother him. Our children started to pick up on my husband's positive responses to negative talk. They would say, "Nana said unkind things about both of you today, but we just changed the subject." My husband calls it redirecting. It seemed to work well for the children, so they kept redirecting her when she starts to talk negative.

There were times after the children had gone on an outing with their nana that they returned home and told us, "Nana got upset with the cashier, but the cashier did nothing wrong." At other times they'd say, "Someone in the store tried to talk to Nana. They were just being friendly, but she seemed offended."

There were times their Nana would buy something for them that they didn't want. When the kids would tell their Nana, "I don't need it," or "It isn't necessary to purchase that item," she would get angry and make a scene.

My mother wasn't able to get over insults or something she felt was offensive. She would often take things the wrong way. She would not take the time to find out from the person what they meant when they made a comment. She would talk about them repeatedly in the car until the children were dropped off. When I opened my front door, she was there to tell the whole story again. Yes, I would listen to her vent about what offended her.

Looking back at those incidents, I now see that they were all red flags. But to avoid confrontations, I would tell my children to agree with her to keep the peace, and by doing this it would keep her happy. The erratic behavior continued for years. Sometimes her actions made me think it was just her way of maintaining control as a parent. I never weighed the possibilities between control issues and mental illness. The behaviors should have raised red flags for us all.

My father was always working. If he wasn't working on his regular job, he was working either inside or outside of the home. He was always doing something besides just "being on the go." Sometimes we don't realize that when we are overly busy trying to keep the peace; it is another way of ignoring the signs. I question myself about the whole situation. How will anyone know if this is a person's personality or actions caused by mental health problems? If you have lived with the person all your life, or have been around a person for a long time, how would you know the difference between what is normal and what is mental health problems?

Our difficult situation has been an eye opener for my husband, children and me. As a result, we communicate more with each other. We are more aware of each other's feelings and actions. We question each other's behavior to get a better understanding of our actions that may seem unusual. We might say, "Why did you say this or that?" or "Why did you do this or that?" This tragedy has brought my immediate family very close. I do believe, we (my husband, my children and I) have learned a lot in many ways. The biggest thing that we have learned is not to be ashamed to speak out on mental health problems because you never know; it just may save a life.

CHAPTER 4

The Pain and Loss

Reality has settled in my oldest sister Marie is not with us. Marie was not just a sister; she was a friend. She walked this earth for forty years and then left. I wish God had given us more time together dying at the age of forty is very young.

Marie was a loving person inside and out. She always seemed to have a smile on her face. My sister's smile will never be forgotten. When she smiled, it was like a light that shined brightly. She could always take a dull moment or situation and brighten it with her smile.

Marie was caring, sharing, loving, respectful, and she had a pleasant personality. She loved being an aunt. She loved spending time with her nieces and nephews. Marie was a jewelry lover. She loved all types of earrings, rings, and necklaces. She loved ribbons, clips and whatever else looked pretty in her hair. Marie had beautiful hair that was long and wavy. She didn't like to have her hair cut, not even a trim.

Mom would trim her hair and explain to us both how doing this helps it to grow. Even though mom said having a small cut at the ends of your hair will help it to improve, I still think Marie was unhappy. The reason why I say that is because ever week she would ask, "Does my hair look like it grown?"

Marie loved to sew. She was in textile classes in high school. I remember her bringing home all kinds of stuff that she had sewn in class. She made pillows, shirts, small blankets and other things. She enjoyed sewing so much that she continued to sew as an adult. She would make clothing for my daughters' teddy bears when they were young. If something was wrong with their teddy bear's clothing, or an eye fell off of a bear's face, my daughters would ask if Aunt Marie could help fix their bears. I would say, "Let's take them to her and see." Somehow she would find a way to fix them. If there were a way to save torn clothing, she would do it.

I remember that one of my girls' teddy bear's eyes were in bad condition, the eyes could not be saved. When she told the girls she couldn't fix the bear's eyes they looked so sad. There were tears in their little eyes. Marie found some buttons and said we could sew these buttons on as eyes. You could see the tears quickly go away, and sad faces turned to smiles.

Marie even sewed buttons on the old teddy bears I had kept into adulthood. I wish I still had them. I don't think it matters how old you are when it comes to having a stuffed animal if it does matter- Oh! Well! I am still a kid at heart.

Marie loved to collect Victorian Dolls. The dolls that she collected were so beautiful and fancy. The dolls would have on Victorian dresses and came with little umbrellas or fancy hats.

Marie would take excellent care of them. She enjoyed collecting them so much that our parents would get her one each year for Christmas. My parents would also buy one for my girls as well.

It hurts knowing I can't just go to my parents' house and visit with my older sister and give her a hug or a kiss on the cheek. It hurts to be unable to receive hugs or a kiss on the cheek from her. I miss hearing Marie's voice and her laughter. I miss seeing the funny faces she would make when someone did something silly. I miss touching her hand or arm to compliment her on her choice of beautiful jewelry she was wearing that day. I just miss having her here on earth and in our lives.

Marie always loved to have her picture taken. She loved the camera, and the camera loved her. She would strike a pose real quick. One hand would be up in the air while the other hand was on her hip or behind her head. She could have been a great model because she never got tired of having her picture taken, even when she began to gain some weight. She had a beautiful smile that showed all of her white teeth. Marie was beautiful with her light-skinned completion. She was also short. I mention her being short because although she was short, she still seemed to stand out. It seemed that everyone who knew her liked her.

Marie had an intellectual disability when it came to schoolwork and trying to comprehend other's actions when it came to social skills. My mom and I helped her with schoolwork, but our mother more than I. My parents got Marie and me a tutor twice a week to help with our homework. Miss Kind was the name of our tutor, who helped us with English and Math homework. I just want to say, when it came to studying for a spelling test or just needing a word spelled, Marie was who you would want to help you. She was an excellent speller, unlike me. I would always have a dictionary nearby.

The extra help was great because we both got a better understanding of our schoolwork. We also made good grades in school. Miss Kind was a wonderful tutor who loved the Lord and brought the best out of children. It was not easy for her to come home after a full-time job as a teacher, and tutor children in the evening. That's what being a Christian is all about, giving up your time for the Lord's work.

My mother and I helped my sister with her social skills. We would talk about things that had happened earlier that day. I would express my opinions, and our mother would give hers. It didn't mean she would agree with what I thought about the situation; it just meant we at least talked about it.

Our mother dressed us alike many times for school and even church. At school, the kids thought we were twins. We liked dressing alike even though we weren't twins. Marie and I were two years apart. She was shorter than me, but she still always let you know she was the oldest. Marie was a very hard worker. We had our chores to do around the house, which Marie always seemed to finish before me. If we didn't do our chores, we would be in trouble; that's for sure.

Our parents were old school kind of people. They disciplined us when need be. They gave us structure and stability. Most important they kept us in the church. I am very thankful that our parents made sure religion stayed first in our lives. If we didn't attend the Catholic Church with our parents, then we would participate in the Mennonite church down the street. Mom would read the Bible to us when we were small kids. My mother and father would get in a circle and hold hands with us and pray. It was only in the past year, before the tragedy, that my parents stopped going to church regularly. My older sister and I turned out to be good kids. My youngest sister Gretchen was one of those kids that had to find out things on her own. I must say that she was a hard worker in school. I can at least say that we all have grown up in church and love the Lord.

Marie always had a kind and loving heart. I think Marie must have thought that God gave me strength, mighty power. Well, at least more strength than what she had.

One day, Marie decided to start telling people about the strength that I possessed. "I am going to get my little sister to beat you up if you keep bothering me," she would say. And the students seemed to believe her. They minded their own business and went on their merry way. I guess they didn't want to get in trouble with the teachers, principals or me.

There was one mean girl, a bully that she and my sister just could not get along with each other. This girl seemed to have some anger issues. One day this girl would not stop bothering Marie. Throughout the whole day, she picked on her. Unfortunately, they had all their classes together. Finally, my sister just got fed up with this girl who was disrespecting her, and she said the magic words, "I'm going to get my little sister to beat you up." The words set this girl off! The girl just automatically switched into fighting mode. It was as if she had heard a boxing ring bell go off in her head. Ding! Ding!

The girl did not care that I was younger than her. No! She did not back down. The girl started yelling and saying harsh words. Marie started walking away from her. She yelled back at her a few times, still walking away. The girl followed her everywhere until a teacher stepped in and told them both to stop or they would have to go to the office. The mean girl backed off, at least for the moment. That girl didn't forget what Marie had said about getting me to beat her up.

I remember my sister coming to me between classes and saying, "a girl is bothering me, and she won't stop. Just to let you know, I told her that I was getting my little sister to beat her up. So this girl wants to fight you at three o'clock today after school."

I said, "What girl!" When my sister told me the name of the girl, I didn't know her. So she said she would point her out to me at lunchtime.

Well, when it was lunchtime, I met up with Marie so she could point her out. When I saw her, my heart dropped down to my belly. I was looking at a big girl, with a big mouth. She was yelling at students in the cafeteria non-stop, and she had big hands. She was a lot taller than my sister and me. I was nothing but a pack of bones compared to her. I had no muscles or any physical qualities to scare off anyone. Now my sister Marie was very petite herself. She was in the same boat as me - a pack of bones and no big muscles.

We were in middle school at this time. Marie was in the eighth grade, and I was in the seventh grade. I don't know why the girl harassed my sister practically every day. But I did know I was caught in the middle and didn't know how to get out of this mess.

The girl spotted us in the lunchroom and said to me, "You're the sister, right?" I managed to nod. "Be ready at three o'clock to get your butt kicked." She continued to say words that were very unkind and unladylike. Then she walked away.

I looked at my sister and said, "She's big, Marie. She could sit on me, and that would be it."

My sister bristled up and said, "Well, you've got to fight. You've got to help me."

"Marie, I'm younger than you. I thought the oldest was supposed to take up for the youngest," I said.

Her reply, "Well, you better get ready!" Then she walked to her class.

My friends had overheard everything in the lunchroom. The next thing I knew, they told me to come into the bathroom with them. Before I knew it, one friend was braiding my hair back, and another had a small jar of Vaseline and was rubbing it all over my face. When they finished with me, I looked like a grease ball.

Soon it was time to go back to class. All I could do was think about everything my friends had told me to do in the bathroom. They said they braided my hair because this mean girl likes to pull hair out of other's skulls when fighting. They also explained why they were putting Vaseline all over my face. It was to protect me from having scratches that would cause me to look ugly until they healed.

For the remainder of the day and in all my classes, I was the topic of discussion. The gossip was about me. It had spread throughout the school. Everyone was waiting for this prime fight to happen. Every time I turned my head, it seemed that someone was there asking if I was ready for the fight or why does the girl want to fight me? They asked me so many times that I decided to ignore everyone. I stopped talking and began praying. I was praying that day!

When the last bell rang, I went to my locker. Some of my friends were standing around waiting for me. "Are you ready," they asked.

"No!" I said. "I still don't know why I'm fighting in the first place." I was scared.

One of the girls asked me what I was going to do just as my sister ran up to me and tapped me on the shoulder. "The girl is outside waiting for you," she said.

I looked at Marie and said, "She's too large to fight." I must have looked terrified because my sister stated that we should go to the principal's office. I quickly agreed, as we ran there to get help, I was praying aloud that the principals would still be there and not somewhere else in the building.

I smiled as we entered and saw both principals standing at the counter. As we were explaining our dilemma, a teacher came. She said, "Girls, your mother is outside by the side door waiting for you." My sister and I had the biggest smiles on our faces as we were told to go to the car. The principals assured us that they would take care of the situation regarding the big fight that was to go down with the mean girl. We both left the office thanking God! Talk about having a prayer answered. God is always on time.

Marie and I ran fast to mom's car and jumped in. When mom asked us if something was wrong, in unison we said, "Not anymore!" I was surprised to find out later that my mom didn't know about the fight. I thought someone had called her, but they hadn't. Mom would pick us up now and then, but why that day? Talk about how God answers prayers quickly!

As we were driving away from the school, I could see the principals talking to the mean girl. When we got home, we told Mom and Dad the whole story. They laughed when we told them that the girl could have sat on us and ended everything. My sister and I used a lot of facial expressions as we told them the story. That night ended up being a fun evening.

I told my sister that night that the next time she got into trouble with a person a lot bigger than her, "don't say I'll get my little sister to beat you up, just tell the principal! I also told her, "But no matter what, I've got your back. We'll solve things together." I stood up for my sister whenever she needed me to. Marie stood up for me too.

After our conversation, we listened to some Michael Jackson music and looked at magazines of the Jackson Family that we had collected. We both enjoyed listening to their music and trying to do the moonwalk. Those were the good old days. At school the next day, we found out that the mean girl got suspended for three days. My sister never had any more problems with her.

Marie and I had a lot of fun growing up together because we are so close in age. I remember when we were smaller, putting a white sheet over our heads, pretending to be a ghost and scaring our mom so bad that she yelled. It was so funny to see her reaction. Afterward, she laughed at herself and us. We did give her a good scare. I remember mom chasing us around the house having fun with Marie and me. Our ages at that time were about seven and nine.

Marie and I even lived together after we graduated high school. My parents built a blue bi-level house on the extra property that they had. It wasn't far from where their first home was. It was pretty nice, feeling like we were on our own. But mom and dad still came over a lot to make sure we kept up with the house chores and the grass.

If we didn't maintain the house cleaning, we got a big earful from both parents. Believe me, Marie and I were on it! If we heard a car pull up into the driveway, the first thing my sister and I said to each other was, "Is your room clean?" If the rooms weren't clean, we would run to our rooms and hurry to put things away before the doorbell rang.

The laughter never seemed to stop. After our parents left, we would look at each other and comment, "That was close." Then things would go back to usual. We would watch television together or play one of my favorite card games; I Declare War.

My little girl Kimora also lived with us. My sister was a wonderful aunt. She would watch her if I had to work late. My parents still continued to help me with my daughter. Kimora was the first grandchild and the first niece in the family. All of them spoiled her. My youngest sister didn't seem to like that at all.

I think she felt that she should have been the only one spoiled by the family. After all, Kimora wasn't my parents' daughter even though they treated her like she was.

I can understand why my little sister would feel like that because she is the youngest out of us three girls. I was the middle child. I was spoiled somewhat by my dad, and that's certainly all right with me. Looking back on everything, I am grateful that my parents accepted my daughter even though I had her out of wedlock. As I mentioned before, my parents were not happy when I told them I was pregnant. It was an embarrassment to the family. But once Kimora was born, my parents loved her as if she were their child. It was a hard pregnancy emotionally. I was depressed, scared, worried, sad, and I felt like a failure. I felt all those bad feelings because deep down inside I knew how much I had disappointed my parents. They were so angry and disappointed with me that they did not call me by my name for months. I was called all kinds of bad names for a long time, and yes, I did answer to all of them.

I realize my parents were hurt and furious, but calling me names hurt deeply. For a time, I was worried that when my baby was born, she might not know my actual name. I thought the bad names would never stop coming from their mouths.

I still love my parents even though they never said they were sorry for the mean words they called me. The word "sorry" seems to be hard for some parents to say to their children, but not for me. I realized early on as a parent that if I said or did something wrong, it was critical to say those particular words, "I'm sorry," regardless of the child's age.

Those words are so important to say when you're in the wrong, even if what you've done is not intentional. It's also important for parents to know that if a child comes home and says the words "I am pregnant," that they don't need to disown or call them bad names. Calling your child bad names is not going to help. It only brings more hurt.

My whole point in sharing this part of my life is to explain how a stressful situation ended up as a blessing, not just to me but also to my family. My parents did a good job raising my siblings and me. My oldest sister Marie and I were well-behaved children. We didn't give my parents any problems. Neither of us ever smoked, did drugs, or drank alcohol. We never went to wild parties and never hung out in the streets. Hanging with the wrong crowd wasn't in our character. The worst thing I ever did in my teenage years was getting pregnant. Now for my youngest sister Gretchen, she was the type who would test my parents. Like an old saying; "She will give you a run for your money."

Even though Marie, baby Kimora and I lived at the blue house, we always respected the fact that our parents built it for us. So we came in at a reasonable time, and we didn't run the streets. We honored our parents regardless of our age.

When we lived in the blue house, there was a young couple that lived across the street from us who always seemed to have problems in their relationship. There would be so much yelling and fussing in the middle of the night. It would wake my sister and me, but little Kimora could sleep through anything. I will never forget the time the yelling and fussing woke both of us up, and we picked up the phone to call the police. We looked out of the window to see what was happening.

We didn't see anything, so we decided not to call but to sit near the window and listen to the screaming and yelling over a bag of microwave popcorn.

That night was so funny. My sister and I couldn't stop laughing. It was better than the television soap, "All My Children." No one got hurt, but there was just a whole bunch of yelling and clothing thrown out the window. Marie and I had a lot of laughs together. It's wonderful to have memories that you can share and still smile. I miss Marie so much.

Marie wasn't only loved by her family but also by a young man of Asian descent. This young man kept my sister smiling. I can't remember his name, but I do remember how much she loved him. I must admit that I didn't think he was her type, but when I saw them together, they looked good. Yes! He was her type after all. When he picked her up for a date, he used his manners. I am very big on manners. My parents are big on manners too!

He made sure he opened and closed the door for Marie. There was, "yes sir" and "no sir" and "yes ma'am" and "no ma'am." Every time my sister and her boyfriend went out he bought something for her: flowers, dinner, movie tickets or jewelry. After each date, my sister always came home talking about the great time she had. She always came home with the biggest smile on her face. Marie liked him a lot. I have forgotten how long they had been dating, but it wasn't long before he pops the question, "Will you marry me?" The next gift she came home with was an engagement ring.

We were shocked but happy for her. I'll never forget the smile on her face. It was priceless. You could see how happy they both were. I told Marie that I would buy the flowers for the wedding. I remember holding something in my hand pretending it was the bouquet of flowers she would hold as she walked down the aisle. It was a beautiful time in her life.

When someone you love asks you to marry them, and you say yes, it's like music to the couple's ears. Sadly, the engagement was called off. My sister was hurt. Watching my sister walk around the house looking so sad, hurt me too. I ached for her. It was hard to see her so sad. It took a little time for her to move forward with her life.

We all knew that although the engagement was off and the relationship was over, she still loved him. I don't think she ever got over him. There would be times I saw her open the ring box and just look at the ring and other jewelry he had bought her. Sometimes she would wear the ring. When I asked why, she would say, "It's my ring, and I feel like wearing it today."

I would say, "That's alright with me," and then I would continue with my day, thinking that the guy missed out on an incredible young lady.

I can go on and on about memories I have of Marie. I always talk about Marie with my husband and children, sharing the good and bad times. It's nice to know I can share my memories with my family along with tears and laughter. It helps keep the memories alive.

If God said to me today that He would give me a few minutes with my oldest sister Marie so that I could tell her what I didn't get a chance to say before she died here on earth, I would want to say so much.

But because I would have only a few cherished moments, I would ask my sister to please listen to a poem that I'd written just for her. The title would be, "There Is No Greater Sister Then You."

There Is No Greater Sister Then You

I love you Marie so much
I miss you, the sound of your voice, your touch
I wish I could hold you close
If only I got one more chance to touch you, for just a moment, I would make it the most
I wish you could stay
My God, please don't make her have to go away
Marie, when God chose us from the start
To be sisters, Boy! Was that smart
Do you remember when we learned how to bake?
Baking cookies, cakes, and pies was fun to make
Each ingredient had to go in just right
Hoping and praying once the food was done it would be out of sight
Laughing and playing together is what we did best
But now I know it is time for you to rest
The love of a sister that I have for you
Will never be matched by anyone else, they will never do
Your beautiful face, your lovely hair and a smile with a glow
You're a blessing, after blessings that no one would understand or know
I am proud to have a sister like you
No one else would ever do
I Love you

I can say that being a sister is something special, but being her sister was so much more than special. I would tell her that I am so grateful God chose us to be sisters. The times we shared growing up will never be forgotten. Thank you for the respect and honor you gave. Thank you for your love, kindness, compassion, and so much more. Thank you for teaching me precious things that I can and will pass down to my children.

I know I would be crying. I always cry when I think of Marie. I know the tears would flow. But I would manage to go on. I would tell her that Mom did not know what she was doing when she shot her. I would tell her to please understand that Mom loves you, but she was sick with mental illnesses.

If I could just turn back the clock and go back in time, I would do it quickly. And when God says, "Marie, it is time to come home with me," I would look at Marie and know that the life she lived on earth was well done. After that we would both hear God say, "Well done, thy good and faithful servant."

And I'd say, "Marie, we'll see each other again because I promise to live my life the way Jesus Christ would want me to live, just like you did. So don't worry. I will never forget what you taught me, and most of all, I will never forget you."

I would give her a big hug and a kiss, holding her so close to me and so very tight. When I hear God speak again, "Marie, it's time," I would say to God, "Thank you, God. Thank you for the time you gave us."

"I'll see you later, Marie. I know you're my angel watching over me." And as I watched her in the sky, I'd blow her a kiss reminding her it was not goodbye; just I'll see you later.

CHAPTER 5

The Test of Faith

I am unable to trust anyone. I feel that if my mother could harm my sister, even though it was not her intention, who then can I trust? The tragedy has made a significant impact on my ability to trust others. So, tell me, wouldn't it be hard for you to trust? If you can't trust the person who brought you into the world, how can you not have a problem with trusting others?

If my father let the lies of another creep into his mind, heart, and soul which ruin our close father-daughter relationship; how can I trust? If my little sister could tell lies that could destroy my reputation, betray me, gossip, disrespect, hurt and cause me so much pain; I spoiled Gretchen and treated her as if she were my daughter. How can I trust anyone? If a brother-in-law, who I loved like a brother welcoming him into the family with open arms; could yell in my face and tell me he didn't ask me to pray for him and didn't need my prayers as he continues to say such mean things; how can I trust?

I still love my mother, father, little sister and brother-in-law despite all of the hurt they've caused. "God, tell me how am I to move on from here? How am I going to be able to trust others?" I am grown and married to a wonderful man who is a great husband and father. I have great, beautiful and respectful children. But the pain of not being able to trust affects the relationship I have with my family.

I understand that my mother's actions were not intentional, but her actions have caused reactions I could never have imagined. I thought my father and little sister would have tried harder to hold on to what family there was left. I didn't just lose my oldest sister Marie and my mother; I lost my father, my little sister Gretchen and my brother-in-law Troy. I realize that I've also lost my three nephews, my little sister's children and my children have lost their first cousins.

My family misses the boys a lot. It's sad because a generation of love and trust gone because of all this. I was feeling all alone, but through all of the turmoil, I turned to my faith. It seemed like everyone who knew me thought I would be mad at God.

At first, I was angry with God. I didn't understand why He would allow this to happen to Marie. I just couldn't understand how God could let my sister die like that. Nobody knows how they will leave this earth, but we all have a date with death. I just felt that my older sister didn't deserve to die like she did. She was a good, caring, respectful person. It's not as if she were a bad person. Maybe I could have understood if she were doing bad things in the streets or had issues with the law but Marie wasn't that kind of person.

I think the hardest thing for me to understand mentally was that my mother pulled the trigger. I had a hard time processing that. I had a hard time understanding that mental illness had caused our mother to do this horrible act.

I couldn't understand why God allowed my mother to have such a terrible mental illness that resulted in her doing something like this. One thing for certain, this tragedy has made me realize who my real friends are. It seemed like I had to define what an actual friend is. There were moments when I had to question myself. Is this person someone who cares about my family and me, or is it just someone being nosey and using my situation to gossip?

Good friends of the family advised my husband and me to go to marriage counseling. With all that was happening, we decided on counseling because it was putting stress on our relationship. We also made the decision that our children would go to counseling. We decided that I would also have individual counseling.

The lives of our children have changed in so many ways since the tragedy, one of my daughters, who was ten years old at the time of the incident, became fearful of everything. She wouldn't go into the bedroom by herself. She was scared of just being alone. She would leave the bathroom door open whenever she used it. It got to be so bad that I would stand outside the bathroom door. If she knew I left, even for a few moments, she would cry. For a while, she couldn't sleep unless I was with her. It seemed like all of the children had issues of one kind or another.

The drastic changes in our lives made me want to give up on life, but I knew I couldn't. I had a family, and they needed me. But looking back, I didn't think I'd be around very long. I didn't think I'd be able to survive. There was so much worry, so much pain and hurt inside. I asked myself, "If I choose to end my life today; what lesson would I be teaching my children?" They would be learning that when life has gotten too hard to endure, just end it. I knew that wasn't right.

After all of the crying and all the questions I was asking God, I just asked Him to help me and help my family. "I look to you, my Lord. I thank you for God's Word (Bible). I stand in faith believing that you are with us as we go through this storm." I knew that even in this horrible situation, God's grace and mercy abounds. Mercy is what I pray that God will give my mother every day of her life. No matter what has happened, she is a child of God.

When you do something wrong, regardless of what it might be or how bad it is, I want you to be encouraged. God is a forgiving God. He is a loving God. We serve a good God. Our Heavenly Father is God of the universe. He created the world. The Bible says, "In the beginning was the Word, and the Word was with God, and the Word was God. He was at the beginning with God." (John 1:1-2.) That is what makes Him so unique. He loves us all the same. His love is unconditional. The Bible says; "For God so loved the world that He gave His only begotten Son, that whoever believes in Him should not perish but have everlasting life." (John 3:16.)

Standing on faith is a big test. I have nothing else to fall back on but my faith. One thing I do know for sure is that if this tragedy is not a test of my faith, then I don't know what is. There are trust issues our family is still going through; God continues to strengthen us more and more each day as we read the Word of God. The Word of God is the Bible, which is truth. The only way to get closer to God and have a close relationship with Him is by reading the Bible. Also, you should be in a good church where you can fellowship with other Christians. I am a child of God, also work in progress.

I have been truly blessed to have a church family that shows so much love and compassion for others. They have helped my family and me to get through this storm in our lives.

My husband and children have always shown me love, but through this storm, in our lives, they have even more. There were kisses on the cheeks, lots of hugs, and they would place notes around the house reminding me of how much they loved me. All I did was cry, if someone said, "Boo," I cried. It got to the point that I was crying out to God non-stop. I felt I deserved an answer. The answer I would get from Christian people who loved me was, "God will use this horrible tragedy so that He will be glorified." I didn't understand, and I responded, "How can this tragedy glorify God?"

The answer I got that some who heard about this tragedy would educate themselves about mental health or want to seek help for themselves or others. Some would want to change their lives for the better, turn their lives over to the Lord because life is short and it's important to have a relationship with our Lord and Savior, Jesus Christ.

I knew deep down inside, no matter what happened, God loved me and had not abandoned me. God promised in Deuteronomy 31:6; "Be strong and of good courage, do not fear nor be afraid of them; for the Lord your God, He is the One who goes with you. He will not leave you nor forsake you." I knew I could trust God because of His Word and the promises He made to us all. I am a child of God. My God cannot lie. No matter what, I know God's word is truth. So with all my heart and all my might, I trust God.

I prayed more to God. I begged God for his help, to keep me in the right state of mind. I cried out to God in such a way that I never had before. I would stay up throughout the night talking, crying, and praying to my Heavenly Father. I guess I was questioning if God could hear me because for a minute I started to have some doubt. However, I knew deep down in my heart, if I took Jesus Christ my Lord and Savior (who is the Lord of all lords and the King of all kings) out of my life, then there was no reason for me to exist. I knew I was at a point in my life that I had never been before.

I wanted to give up on life, but still having to face reality, I knew this would not make things any better. I was ready to die. It was hard to come to the realization that I felt I had failed my oldest sister. I wasn't there to protect her like I did when we were younger. To me, it was still my responsibility to protect her, no matter how old she was. You always hear people say to each other, "I got your back." Do they mean it? Or is it just a saying that sounds cool. My sister needed me, and I wasn't there. I didn't have her back. I never thought she would need protection from our mother. What person would believe they need to protect a sibling from a mother who loved them?

I wish the truth about my mom's mental illnesses had been said to me so that the family as a whole could have helped to avoid the tragedy. I love my mother dearly, and I feel the family failed her. If there had been open communication and there hadn't been such secrecy, this tragedy would never happen.

Gretchen and Troy told me that my mother did not want me to know about her mental illnesses. Tell me how someone could let my mom, in her state of mind; make such a decision by just saying that she didn't want me to know about her mental illnesses. There has to be open communication among family members when it comes to particular kind of health care decisions.

I can't imagine what my mother is feeling, now that she is on the correct medications. Mom has now come to the point of knowing what she has done, killing her first born adult daughter she loved? The pain is something she has to live with every day of her life. She also has to live with the pain of being unable to walk, something most of us take for granted. I wonder what my mother is thinking about as she goes to sleep at night, as she lays in her bed, not in a hospital, but in prison. One thought I know she has to have is "Why didn't my family try harder to help me?"

I remember my mother begging in the emergency room to have her head checked. She shouted it a few times to the nurses and doctor. It was a cry for help. She needed help, but no one listened. My mother asked if they would check her head, which meant she wanted testing done. She sensed something wasn't right. I asked myself if the nurses and doctors were somewhat responsible for this tragedy. The first thing they thought of was to put her in a mental hospital for an evaluation. "The family physician would have to admit her," is what the nurse said in the emergency room.

My mother was not expecting to end up in a mental hospital. She thought her cry was heard and a neurologist would give her an examine, which did not happen. I feel that my mother was not heard. I thought one important part of a doctor's job was to listen and understand his or her patient. That is my opinion; everyone has the right to an opinion.

I'm not a doctor, but I do believe the patient should be heard. What went wrong? Was it that my mom put her faith in man? Or was it our faith in man? Should we have come together as a family and prayed right there in the emergency room? Would the outcome have been different? Was my faith too little? Why didn't the family stay together throughout this whole ordeal? Why? Why? Why? So many why's waiting to be answered. I could almost hear God saying, oh ye of little faith, but I love you. God loves me, and I love Him.

I cried out again and again. "I can't handle this! I feel like I'm in water up over my head and I am sinking! God, this storm in my life is more than I can handle."

It's amazing how God works. He delivered peace, the peace that passes all understanding. I knew that no matter how big the storm, no matter how high the waves became, no matter how many times the wind currents tried to knock me down, I was to stand on my faith and stand on God's promises. He is with me and has reminded me many times through and after the tragedy that I am not alone or on my own in this world. He is with me. The Bible says in Philippians 4:13; "I can do all things through Christ who strengthens me."

If that means I have to be the black sheep of the family, then so be it. But God said that I am not alone. It is not to say I'll stop crying. It just means that I'm not crying alone. My dad and little sister Gretchen have not been in my life up to this time (February 2015), which has been five years. I cannot visit my mother in prison because she doesn't want me to see her in that place. God said that I'm not alone. I don't have my big sister to talk too or share special moments with anymore. But God said that I am not alone.

At this time in my life, I choose to live a purpose filled life with God's love and his bountiful blessings! I refuse to allow the devil to take hold. I refuse to let the deceiver, the author of confusion, and the father of lies to get any glory out of this tragedy.

The Bible says in John 8:44; "You are of your father the devil, and the desires of your father you want to do. He was a murderer from the beginning and does not stand in the truth because there is no truth in him. When he speaks a lie, he speaks from his own resources, for he is a liar and the father of it."

"I rebuke him in the name of the Father, the Son, and the Holy Spirit! In Jesus Christ's name, I pray, Amen." I am a child of the highest God, which means I am royalty. God has not, and will not, fail my family or me.

God never promised that life on earth would be filled with happiness all the time. He never promised that we wouldn't experience pain or endure hardship in life. But one great thing I know, God promised never to leave nor forsake us. We don't have to go through it alone. He is my strength! God can be your strength too, but only if you open your heart and allow Jesus Christ into it, and accept Him into your life as your Lord and Savior.

CHAPTER 6

Life's Encouragement

Think of how many times people have put you down, disrespected you, or hurt your feelings in some way. Think carefully, did you forgive each of them? If not, why not? Why would God forgive you if you cannot forgive others? In Matthew 6:15 it reads; "But if you do not forgive men their trespasses, neither will your Father forgive your trespasses."

I have had a lot of people come up to me and ask me if I forgave my mother and my response to them was "Yes! I have forgiven my mother." I would also get questions from others asking if I would ever talk to my little sister Gretchen again after she had hurt my family and me so bad. My answer to that is "Yes!" I had people ask me about my feelings towards my father. They wanted to know after he had disowned my family and me for no good reason, would I forgive him? My answer was, "I already have!"

I will not allow bitterness to enter my heart. Jesus was beaten, disrespected, falsely accused, mocked and so much more to the point he was put on the cross and crucified. He had every right to give up on us and choose not to forgive us of our sins, but Jesus Christ did not become bitter. He showed all of us love by going through with his crucifixion and dying on the cross for all of our sins. Now for the people who did him wrong he showed them love by saying to his father, "Father, forgive them because they know not what they do." (Luke 23:34a) Who do you know that could have said the same words like Jesus did to his father after going through the pain and hurt he endured. I can say I don't know anyone like that. Jesus had every right to curse his accusers, to yell, to disrespect them, and even to have hatred in His heart towards them, but he didn't. He stayed on the cross until his death. If Jesus Christ wanted to get off the cross, he could have called on the angels to help him. There is no greater love. His love is unconditional.

Forgive is a strong word. It's not easy to forgive when you've been hurt so bad by someone. When you look at the situation Jesus was in, you have to ask; "What excuse do I have not to forgive others?" There is no excuse. I can forgive the ones who hurt me. In fact, we are required to forgive. Jesus tells us in Matthew 6:14 that if we forgive others, He will forgive us.

Through all the pain, I thank God for reminding me that He is with me. I regularly pray and give thanks. I Thessalonians 5:17-18 tells us; "Pray without ceasing, in everything give thanks; for this is the will of God in Christ Jesus for you." In fact, I was calling on God so much that I would start my prayers by saying, "It's me again. Sorry to bother you." If I have a headache, worry, concern, or question, I called on God. I still cry at times. I cry because the family is not together for holidays, birthdays, or just plain ole get-togethers. I love them and miss them all, even though our get-togethers were not always good.

I know when it's my time to see the Lord He is going to have a lot of questions for me. I'm sure you're wondering why I say that. It's because I just think I probably worked his nerves.

My pastor's wife told me that God never gets tired of hearing from us. I hope not because I don't have a father here on earth to share with or talk too. So I talk to my Heavenly Father all the time. I am now at the point that I can talk to him anywhere. I can truly say my relationship with God has gotten stronger than ever. I have found that God brings clarity and focus to our lives. Clarity and focus are something that we all need in life. We need to have clarity in our lives to live the purpose of why we are here on earth. We also need to stay focus and make sure that we follow through to finish what God wants us to do. That's why we need God directing our lives, and we need to be following him.

My family and I are still coping with stuff that happened in the past. I want people to know when a loved one is murdered: they are dead, and a part of you die too. When your loved one goes to prison for life, it's like your having a death sentence and a part of you is lost too. The reason why I say that is because even though they suffer, in some ways we hurt too. I want people to understand that it is so important to know that mental illness should not be considered a "silent disease." We, the people, should not be embarrassed to speak out and let others know that we care and want to find ways to help the ones who are dealing with mental illnesses. When someone in the family is facing a physical disease or crisis of some kind, wouldn't we find a way to help them? The answer is yes. In fact, we would go out of our way to help the person that we love and cherish.

Then why wouldn't we do the same when it comes to mental health issues? The family should find ways to help the person who is facing mental health problems just as they would if that person has a physical illness; for example, cancer. In these types of situations, family and close friends need to come together and be a team. A family coming together to work as a team means that everyone gets educated about the illness or diseases that their loved one is facing. Everyone should work together to help the person in need. By doing so, some family members are better in recognizing problems that other family members might not see to help get their loved one the proper care they need as soon as possible. It should not be about the fear of what others might say or think. It's all about showing love and respect to your loved one. Working together as a team to help the person you love is a great way of showing your love towards them.

If the individual did not have immediate family members to go to, they should reach out to others in the family, the pastor, church members, friends or someone who could help them get the appropriate medical care. Also, it is important that our Government and the leadership of the United States get involved in funding more for mental health.

In many letters that I've written to my mom, I reminded her of the unconditional love I have for her. I wonder what she thought when she read those letters. I wish I could have seen her face on how she reacted about the letters; I reminded her of how much God loves her too. I told her how God was able to use Paul while he was in prison. I just wanted my mother to know God loves her, regardless of the sin she has committed. I wanted my mom to know that God had not abandoned her. I always remind her in the letters that she is not alone in her prison cell. She has God and the marching angels there with her.

My mother is a Christian. She repented of her sins after she received the correct medications that helped her come back to reality and the right state of mind.

It is so hard for me to imagine the heartbreak, pain, hurt and shock she experiences. I am sure that at times my mother sits in her cell trying to comprehend what she did. Who wouldn't!

She sits in her prison cell serving punishment for murdering her adult child with physical and mental disabilities. My mother cried out for help before this tragedy took place by asking for a CAT scan in the emergency room. No CAT scan was given then or at least within the first week of her stay at the mental hospital. She sits in her cell hoping and praying that there is a miracle out there that will release her from the prison walls that surround her. Sadly to say, the prison walls of sinful thoughts in her mind of what she did to her adult daughter that ended her life can never go away. It's like she is in prison: within a prison; the prison of the mind and cell.

Why must a woman, who sadly did take her child's life but who also had severe mental health issues, have to spend the rest of her life in prison? I just wonder, did the professionals do everything correctly? Has anyone checked to make sure if anything more can be done by professionals to help prevent such a tragedy? How can this tragedy be avoided? I don't want anyone else to experience this pain and hurt. I am not in the medical field, but I do feel there should be a way to make sure a tragedy like this doesn't happen again. I just wonder if a registered nurse and case worker should be involved in a patient's life for at least six months to a year after a psychiatric hospital stay. By having the home health care services through mental health would also help create more jobs. There is a lack of funds for mental health, but if having those services could help save lives, I hope people will come together and find ways to provide funding.

Marie had a lot of medical and mental issues she was dealing with also my mother was Marie's caregiver. Needless, to say the doctor knew that our mother was the person who had to make sure my sister took her medications. My oldest sister could not live alone. Did the mental facility where my mom stayed seek out, or suggest other agencies, local, state or government that could step in on my sister's behalf? I don't know. If they had done so, could my sister's life have been saved, and my mother prevented from going to prison?

I strongly feel that this tragedy could have been avoided in so many ways. I can't see this tragedy just being a mistake committed by one person, but only God can be the judge of that. I question if the trained professionals ignored my mother's cries for help? Again, I don't know. Now the other thing, maybe her cries were heard, but the staff wasn't fully trained to deal with her situation. We need more trained professionals to get more education in mental health. Yes, that also means in the emergency rooms at hospitals. Again, that goes back to the need for more funding for mental health.

Once my mother was placed in the psychiatric unit there were also red flags everywhere that were not paid attention too. She told the staff that she is a caregiver for her oldest daughter. My mother was told by her doctor, "You haven't been taking good care of yourself. As a result, this caused you to have these mental illnesses." This statement my mother shared with me shortly after being released from the psychiatric unit. So I just wonder, why would they continue to allow her to watch my older sister as her caregiver if she couldn't take care of herself? When I think about that statement, I think about my sister. Shouldn't an agency have stepped in and removed her from their home?

If someone had called and asked me if my sister could come to my house to live, I would have done it in a heartbeat. No problem, Maria would be welcome in my home. To my knowledge, there were no home health aide, caregiver, nurses (LPN or RN), or caseworker visiting the home to make sure my mother was taking her medicine and giving my older sister her medication. There should be state law requirements for caregivers to follow when there diagnosed with a mental health illness so that their love one will have protection as well as themselves. I think if this became law for anyone who is discharged from a mental health unit; just maybe our prisons wouldn't be so full. Again, this is just my opinion.

Please explain to me how this horrible burden of guilt that is on my mom is totally her fault? I can't believe she is entirely responsible. I remember the day my mother said she was fighting for her life. I didn't know what she meant at that time. I'm not sure if she understood what she meant. Now I understand, you can't have a good life without being in the right state of mind. You can't have a real life when you don't know who you are, or what your purpose is in life.

To my mother, I say, "Be of good courage. God is directing you and guiding you. He will see you through." My mom may be in a prison cell, but my God is bigger than any prison cell. He will see her through.

To the medical staff that worked with my mother before the tragedy, I say that if you know, you made a mistake and failed my mom and older sister, please go to God and repent. Sorry to sound like John the Baptist, but I want to let you know that I am not perfect. We all make mistakes, but it's important to repent when we do. The first step is to ask for forgiveness after admitting the wrongdoing. You may have a problem with authority here on earth, but the truth is, God's the ultimate authority. Your concern should be with answering to him. Where will you spend eternity?

We are to have a fear of God in our hearts. For Christians, this means having reverence and respect in our hearts for God. For the unbeliever, it means knowing there will be separation from him. But we will all have to answer to God.

I always say that if it weren't for God, I wouldn't be where I am today. I may not be the prettiest lady, the wealthiest person, the most famous person on earth, or whatever the world may consider is "being the best of," but one thing I do know, I am blessed in every way. I have Jesus Christ in my life!

I've always said, "things could have been worse" and it could have been. My children could have been killed. They tried to visit my mom the day before the tragedy, but she wouldn't allow them to come in the house. If my mother had let them in the door with that state of mind, it could have been the last time I saw them. But God!! If it had not been for the Lord keeping watch over them, they might not be here today for me to hug. I give God all the praise and glory.

The verse that comes to my mind is from Matthew 11:28-29. "Come to Me, all you who labor and are heavy laden, and I will give you rest. Take my yoke upon you and learn from Me, for I am gentle and lowly in heart, and you will find rest for your souls." I just want to encourage you to open your heart to Jesus Christ and make Him your Lord and Savior.

CHAPTER 7

Letters of Love

It is so important to show love in all situations because that's what Jesus Christ would do. It is so easy to show love when everything is going great. But when things are going wrong, we still need to love. God taught us how to love in the good times and bad. God sent His only begotten Son to die for our sins. That's love! God knew the pain His Son would endure on earth, and He still showed love by allowing His Son to give His life for us. God knew His Son's death would save all of us from death and offer eternity with Him. God wasn't selfish. He gave us His Son. God has an amazing love for us all. It's amazing how love can heal any broken heart.

Looking back over the past few years, I come to realize that love can conquer all. People wonder how I can say this after all that has happened. I say it because love is the tool for healing. I choose to love. I do know love works.

When this tragedy first happened, I knew deep down inside that God was in control and that He was aware what is best for us. I had mixed emotions about love. Being able to continue to love was questionable. But now, after a time of healing, I can say for sure that without love in your heart, you have nothing. In 1 Corinthians 13, God tells us the characteristics of love. I focus on those characteristics; what it means to love even my enemies. Although my mother harmed my sister, she is not my enemy. She is my mom, and I love her.

Someone asked me an interesting question after my mom's trial. They asked if I have a good mother. They asked, "Why would a mother do such a horrible thing to their child." I didn't answer the question at the time. I couldn't. I can now. She was a good mom. She wanted the best for her children. She raised us, kids, the right way. I remember things that my mom would do when I was younger I did not understand. I now know that her behavior had a lot to do with her mental illnesses.

It is not easy being a mother. A manual on being a mother does not come out of the womb along with the baby when it's born. I wish it did. Maybe then the job of being a mother would be a lot easier.

Being a Christian mother is a lot like being a gardener. When we plant flowers, we must plant correctly to make sure the plant grows. It has to be well-rooted to grow to full maturity. For a plant to thrive, it has to be healthy and well-rooted. It is the same for raising a child.

Step 1: You must put the seed into a small flowerpot with fertilized soil. Make sure you cover the seed well with the dirt.

Step 2: You must put some water into the flowerpot on top and around the seed. You must be careful not to over water. Too much water can ruin the foundation of the plant.

Step 3: Make sure you place the pot in the right area of the house, preferably near a window so it can get the proper amount of sun. The sun is a big part of helping the plant to grow.

Step 4: Now watch and see how a seed turns into a well-rooted plant. It is important for the plant to be well-rooted to grow.

Step 5: It is important to remember as the plant grows that you will have to change the pots from small, to medium and then to large, this is called transplanting the plant. When to transplant will depend on the size and maturity of the roots.

Step 6: Remember you will have to continue to water it and make sure it is getting enough sun.

When you follow these steps, the result is a beautiful, sturdy, well-rooted and thriving plant. Just as the plant needs soil, which helps the foundation, the child needs a firm foundation: Jesus Christ.

The plant growth is important, so it needs to be in a right size pot with no cracks in it to make sure it doesn't lose soil or water. The plant cannot grow without the proper amount of water and the right amount of sunlight; this is the way we as Christians (children of God) also function. Mother's take care of us as babies by feeding us the Word of God. They tell us Bible stories, take us to church, teach us to sing songs about the Lord and teach us to read the Bible. The mother waters the seed (the baby spirit) that God has placed into her care, which is vital to a child's growth. How well he's rooted in the Word of God helps determine how he grows; this does not mean the child will not lose sight of God's teachings or try to ignore God's instructions when he is older. But the Bible tells us to, "Train up a child in the way he should go: and when he is old, he will not depart from it." (Proverbs 22:6) Children rebel, but often their story of rebellion becomes a testimony of God's redemptive power. Their story becomes a learning tool to help others not to make the same mistake they did.

When my sisters and I were young, we went to a Catholic Church; this was how my parents watered our spirit with God's word. When we were older, my parents allowed us to go to the Mennonite Church while they remained in the Catholic Church. Again, our spirits were being watered with God's Word. My mother did her part when it came to being a Christian mother, and I believe that. She did the best that she could. My mom lost her mom when she was fourteen years old. She didn't have the example of how to be a mother, but God brought her through and taught her. Yes, she made mistakes, but she had to learn from them. The error I am talking about was from when we were younger.

Here is the letter of love I send to my mother to let her know how much I love her and how much she is loved.

Dear Mom,

We all miss you very much. Mom, I want you to know that I am not upset with you about the tragedy anymore. God healed that open wound that I had for so long. I want you to know Mom, I honor and respect you. I honor you by praying for you every day. I honor you by telling your grandchildren how much you love them. I honor you with encouraging words that hopefully put a smile on your face when I send you cards or letters.

I want you to know you are not a horrible person. You are a child of God. God has washed away your sins and cleansed you. God has created a clean heart within you. Mom, you have a spirit with the word of God written all over it. God's word is pierced into your heart.

Mom, you wrote a beautiful letter on God's grace. In that letter, you said that it was His grace that saved all sinners. When I read the letter, I knew you were in the right state of mind by having the correct medications to help you. I knew God had made sure you did not forget who He was and what He means to you.

Love, your daughter

I've written many letters to my mom. I wrote my mother a letter thanking her for teaching me about the Lord and making sure I stayed in the church. Now that I have six children of my own, I make sure they all stay in the church and are grounded in the Word. I am so thankful for being taught who Jesus Christ is at an early age. I thank God for all the Sunday school teachers and pastors that helped me stay rooted in the Word of God. I am very thankful for the pastors and their families that God has use them as a vessel to teach me.

I am thankful for the pastor and his family that is in our lives right now. I love my church family and our beautiful church.

This letter of love I send to my father.

Dear Dad,

I have never stopped loving you. Dad, I love you with all my heart. I have full respect for you, and I will never stop honoring you. In the Bible, it says to honor your mother and father. It is one of the commandments, and I honor you. Guess what; I want you to know that I have been honoring you through prayer. I pray for you every day, regardless of whether you are in my life or not. I honor you by telling my children about the things you taught me such as how to chop wood. I remember how I would go outside and help you cut, stack and make a fire in the wood stove.

I honor you by sharing our driving stories. I've told them the age I started driving and that you taught me to drive. By the way Dad, your second granddaughter is now driving! Dad, I don't like to see you missing out on the joy of seeing your grandchildren growing up and all because you believe lies. I think it's so sad, and it cheats you out of being the grandfather that God wants you to be. Also, it takes time away from the children being with you. Time is precious and needs to be respected.

The children are growing, and you are missing out on their special years, just being kids, having fun and learning new things all the time. We miss you a lot, Dad. Our big dog misses going out on car rides with you. Dad, remember how you always called her your road buddy. Well, now I've been taking her out. But you were consistent; you took her out pretty much every day.

Please stop believing lies. You know you're wasting precious time. Time is something you don't want to lose. Dad, we want you to know that you are truly loved unconditionally by your grandchildren, your daughter, and son-in-law. We would never hurt you or the family in any such way or form.

Love, your daughter

This letter of love I send to my brother-in-law and nephews.

Dear Troy and Nephews,

I love you guys and miss you dearly. I pray that you are all doing well. I pray for you all a lot. I pray that God will bless you and keep you under His wing of protection. Troy, I just want you to know how much the family and I truly appreciate you and the work that you do in the Army, keeping our country safe, and defending others. I still have full respect for you. I was hurt pretty badly by you, but God is a great healer. I hope you let the boys know that we wish things were a lot different. I wish they could see their first cousins again. We would love to talk to you guys over the phone. You are in my thoughts and prayers.

Love, your sister-in-law, and aunt

This letter of love I send to my little sister.

Dear Gretchen,

I love you and hope one day you will understand how much God, in heaven, loves you. It will be hard to forget the pain and hurt you caused. Although it has hurt our family, I still have unconditional love for you and wish you the best in life. There are scars that you caused our family, but we love you. The trust factor is still being worked on, which could take awhile. God can fix our trust issues over time.

Thank you so much for sending me the letter that I assume is an apology. I know our family wasn't raised to say "I am sorry" when we do something wrong. You were able to admit you were wrong. That is not easy to do, but I respect you for saying it. I know that our parents didn't say the word sorry very much if at all, but it needs to be said and shown.

I don't understand, if your letter was an apology, why didn't you leave your address and phone number so that I could contact you? You even said that it was alright if I didn't want to talk to you ever again. I don't think Jesus would want me to be like that. Jesus would not do that. Yes, the trust is broken. What I mean is because of the pain, lies and hurt, there was so much damage done to our family and friends relationships. My family and I have a hard time trusting you and others. That doesn't mean God can't fix it over time.

I wish I knew how to heal the pain you are going through within your heart. Whatever you have locked inside you, whatever spiritual bondage you carry inside of you, needs to be taken to Jesus! He can heal your pain and any other struggles. I must say there are some things I don't agree with in your letter. You said our father never loved our mother. Dad loves our mother deeply, and he loves his children too. Yes, he was very busy; working a lot but that is what a father often does to take care of his family. I'm sure he wishes; that he could have spent more time with the family, but don't hold that against him. Dad is a good husband, and he is not cheating on mom. He honors his marriage and loves his children. Our dad did the best he could as a father. No, he wasn't perfect but who is? Only Jesus was perfect. I know it was painful when our parents weren't there for the special occasions in our lives, our weddings for example, but they have to live with that for the rest of their lives. Just remember, that was their choice.

I don't understand why they did not come to either of our weddings, but I do feel like there were some mental health issues involved with that. I just want you to know, mom and dad love you and your family very much too. They are so proud of you and what you have done well with yourself.

You going into the military to serve our country was like the biggest talk from our parents. If someone came to visit, or one of them was on the phone with a friend, they would brag about you and how well you were doing in the military. Dad and mom are so proud that you finished college.

Again, they did not come to see you walk on stage for your college degree, but I want you to know they were so proud of you. They tell people about you all the time.

We all are proud of you for all the accomplishments you have made through life. I am sure you will have more as you continue to move forth in your life.

I'm sure you didn't realize this, but no matter what I suggested to Mom or Dad to do in certain situations or if I told them to do something a certain way; they would not listen to me. If you said to them to do something a certain way, they would agree to do it your way. Even if you suggested the same thing that I said, to them, it sounds better out of your mouth. I felt I could not make them proud, but you did. I am not holding that against them or you. I used to cry about it, but God showed me that it's not about my parents or me; it's about our Heavenly Father.

Parents are not perfect. They make mistakes too. I had my talk with mom. I did most of the talking and told her how I felt. I told her I didn't think she loved me. I'm sure that probably hurt her feelings a lot to hear those words come out of my mouth. Mom responded in a weak voice, "I always loved you." And that is what I hold on to, not the past.

I told my therapist I thought my relationship with Dad had been close since I was a little girl. Now, because he believes the lies, he won't give me the time of day.

He won't even let me show him that the lies aren't true. I guess our relationship was not as close as I thought. The pain of coming to that conclusion hurts a lot because our relationship may never be the same again. My children probably have lost their grandfather forever. I hope and pray that whatever is causing you to be mean, sad, or just to push love ones away, please turn it over to Jesus Christ so He can heal you. Please, whatever it is, let it go.

I truly believe God has something special for your life, but it starts with healing. Past hurts have to heal before you can go on with your future. Marie is in heaven with our little sister who died earlier. I don't think they would want this kind of pain, hurt and suffering happening in our family or having the attitude of "just doing me." It's just us left out of the four sisters.

I guess I am also trying to figure out what I have done to hurt you so badly that you would hurt my family and me. I love you so much. Sometimes I would treat you as if you were my daughter. That is why mom would yell at me and say, "She is not your child, so don't treat her like that."

My husband respects you and your husband very much. He loves your boys just as much as I do. Little sister, I just want you to know that even though you have hurt me pretty badly, I will always love you. I love you with all my heart. I still tell my children stories about when we were their ages. I will continue to share stories with them.

Sometimes, if I say your name, it brings tears to their eyes. They have had to endure the same pain and hurt that I went through, but those tears don't mean they haven't forgiven you. They have and still do, love you. The children miss their first cousins and know that they may never see them again. I think this is so sad and hurtful.

Please let the boys know how much we love and miss them. I truly believe love conquers all. I just don't know how long it will take for that love to conquer.

I don't have to give you my address and number because you already know it. If God speaks to you and says it's time for us to sit down and talk with a therapist or a third party, let me know.

I sincerely wish you and your family the best in life. Also, I want God to bless you in every way that He chooses. When I say bless, I am not speaking only of money. Remember, if you don't have love you have nothing. I pray that God will bless you with joy, happiness, meekness, peace, love and a lot more. God loves you all, and we do too. Be Blessed!!!!

CHAPTER 8

Life

When I think about everything that I have gone through in my, life; I wonder how I made it through. Dealing with so much and going through a lot of pain, I am amazed at how I continue to press on. Life is not easy. I remember when I was younger how I wanted everything to be easy. I did not want to have to work hard for anything. When someone would ask me to do something for them, my first question would be, "Is this hard work?" I just thought who would want to go through the pain or suffering to get something if they don't have too. My dad would always say that nothing comes easy in life. My mother would always say that nobody owes you anything. Both of them would always say that if you want something you have to work for it. I stand by those statements even with my children. Right now it will take a lot of work from each of us. My question now is, "How do I make our family a family again?" I can't! I can't go back in time to get my mother the proper help that could have prevented this tragedy from ever happening. I can't bring my older sister back to life. I can't force my father to talk to me when I have reached out, and he continues to reject my family and me. I can't make my little sister stop being mean and doing mean things to others and myself. There is nothing fair in this situation, but God never said one word in the Bible about being fair. I do know for sure God can fix any situation but it's on his time.

Maria's death and how she died has broken me in so many ways. I still cry even though it was five years ago. I cry when I am thinking about the bad memories. Sometimes I cry because I miss making good memories. I am not the same person that I was years ago. I thought just being a Christian and drawing closer to the Lord would be life changing. This tragedy and all that came with it has taken me to another level on how I look at life. People would say to me that whatever doesn't kill you makes you stronger! I would say, 'That is not true!' One day a close friend of mine told me that it's all right to cry, but don't forget to praise God in your sorrow. I just looked at her and asked why I would give God or anyone else praise. She said, "Because He is God, Wonderful Counselor, Jehovah, Teacher and so much more. God knew what was going to happen before it happened because He is the alpha and omega." All I kept saying in between her giving me this speech was why. She finally said, "I don't know why this had to happen, but we have to trust God no matter what." Deep down inside I was thinking, trusting God is what I have always done. I just didn't understand that if God knows the beginning and the end, why he didn't stop it. My friend responded, "God was there with your sister, as well as the angels. You must believe that." I prayed so hard that night before I went to bed. I fell asleep praying. God showed me in a dream that his angels were there in the room with my older sister, but I never got a reason why he allowed it to happen. I just know I must trust Him. I will trust him. I remember waking up the next day, and I could hear a song playing over and over again in my head called, "Love Lifted Me" this was my older sister's favorite song. We used to sing this song at the Mennonite Church that we used to go to when we were kids. That song stayed in my head for a few days, off and on. I knew for sure God was speaking to my heart. I knew what he was saying to me was that I needed to move forth. I must live life. I realized the statement that was made about what doesn't kill you makes you stronger is true!

Guess what? I am stronger! I can hold my head up high and give testimony to as many people who are willing to listen. No, I wasn't able to save my sister or even my mother, but if God opens doors that no man should close for me to speak out to help other families, this could save a life or lives, then something good came out of this tragedy. I do pray that something good will come out of this because I don't want my sister's death to just be in vain. God knows my heart! I will be speaking out on mental health, guns, hospital procedures, open family communication, and faith. A person's faith can help them get through the hardest times in their life. I can at least say "if it wasn't for my faith, husband, children, church family and friends, I truly don't think I would be alive today."

In conclusion, I just want to say that this tragedy could have happened to anyone's family. I believe that working together as a family to help a person with mental health can decrease these tragedies. We need more medical staff being trained on how to handle mental health issues. We need ongoing emergency room staff training once a month or more. We need to have a psychiatrist in the emergency room, not just an on-call person. All counties should have mental health hospitals for in and outpatient treatment. The word 'shortage' in mental health care should not be allowed. The government needs to stop cutting the funding for mental health. This kind of financing is a must have. There is no reason why the prisons are being filled up with people who should be in mental health hospitals to truly get the care that is properly needed for their situation. There should be a law made for caregivers who have mental health issues and are taking care of a loved one. I would like this caregiver's law to be named after my sister. We need to make sure that caregivers get the proper permission from their doctors allowing them to continue to care for their loved ones. The most important thing about creating this law is to keep everyone safe.

I just want everyone to know, that through hail and high waters, God has truly been there for me. In some way, somehow God has reminded me that I am not walking this journey alone. I feel that if you are going through a heavy-duty storm in your life and you just don't know what to do, call on Jesus Christ, Lord and Savior and He will get you through. Now, remember, I never said it would be easy, but just know you don't have to go through this alone. Singing praises to God any time of the day also seems to help me. There were days I just needed answers on things that I would hear regarding my mother situation. I went into the Holy Bible to get answers. I wanted to know how God would deal with this. The closer you draw near to God, the closer He will draw to you. Looking up Bible scriptures in the middle of the night when I can't sleep because I am so worried about my mother being in prison, it soothes me. I can say losing sleep to spend time with the Lord is worth it. I guess you can call it my 'upper room.' The great thing about reading the Word of God and praying to him is that you can do it any time of the day. God never says 'leave me alone.' I was always saying, 'God it's me again' because I would feel like a burden to Him. The truth is, we are not a burden. God wants us to have a close relationship with him. He wants us to know we can turn to Him any time of the day or night. God loves each and every one of us. There is no greater love.

I hope this book has been a blessing to you. I hope this book will give you a different outlook on mental health so that you all will be willing to stand with me to have changes made for the better within our communities. Please stand with me to create this Caregiver Law. Your voice needs to be heard by the state representatives and senators. Every community is affected when it comes to mental health. Mental health illness is not a Black, White, Latino, or any other race or even a poor or rich thing; we can all be affected by this. So, let's work together to make a change.

ABOUT THE AUTHOR

The author's goal in life is to live the way Jesus Christ intended. She enjoys sharing the Word of God with others. She shares her wisdom and experiences in life in hopes to inspire the lives of others.

Printed in the United States
By Bookmasters